How to Make Your Dreams Come True

Also by Mark Forster and published by Help Yourself

Get Everything Done
And Still Have Time to Play

How to Make Your Dreams Come True

Mark Forster

HELP YOURSELF

First published in Great Britain in 2002

10 9 8 7 6 5 4 3 2 1

British Library Cataloguing in Publication Data
A record for this book is available from the British Library

ISBN 0 340 78629 9

Typeset by Avon Dataset Ltd, Bidford-on-Avon, Warks

Printed and bound in Great Britain by
The Guernsey Press Co. Ltd, Channel Isles

Hodder & Stoughton
A Division of Hodder Headline Ltd
338 Euston Road
London NW1 3BH

To Lucy

Thou waitest for the spark from Heaven! and we,
Vague half-believers of our casual creeds,
Who never deeply felt, nor clearly will'd,
Whose insight never has borne fruit in deeds,
Whose weak resolves never have been fulfill'd;
For whom each year we see
Breeds new beginnings, disappointments new;
Who hesitate and falter life away,
And lose to-morrow the ground won to-day –
Ah, do not we, Wanderer, await it too?

Matthew Arnold, from
'The Scholar Gypsy'

Contents

Acknowledgements

I would like to thank all my clients and the many people who have used my Goal Achievement Methods in their own lives for their feedback, suggestions and stories.

I particularly wish to acknowledge the constant support and help that I have had in the writing of this book from my wife Lucy, my coach Rachel Pryor, and my thinking partner Katie Rowland.

Introduction

One of the questions anyone reading this book is likely to ask is, 'Is it real?' By which they will mean, 'Did these dialogues really happen when they were supposed to?', 'Was the first draft of the book really written in nineteen days?', 'Did the events mentioned really happen in the way described?' and above all, 'Did the author really have no idea how the book was going to turn out when he started it?'

The answer to all these questions is 'Yes.' This book itself is an example of the message that it teaches – that when we learn to give priority to the workings of our unconscious minds we can trust them not to let us down. This book is the record of how I stopped struggling to work against my own feelings, learned to listen to what my mind was telling me and started to let my life happen rather than struggle to force it. The only way the book has been changed since the first draft was written is as a result of minor editorial amendments and additions, such as chapter headings and a couple of additional articles, which seemed necessary to develop some of the themes.

It is customary in introductions to say something about the reasons for writing a book. But in this case you will find no fewer than four versions at different places in the book. If you want to read the 'official version' now you will find it on page 154.

Opening scenario

I am working in my office in my castle looking out over a magnificent panoramic view over a bay with yellow sand and a blue sea. I am enjoying the warm sunny climate and the wonderful luminous quality of the light.

My office is a large airy room with a stone floor and walls with tapestries hanging on them. I have a sense of spaciousness, calm and purposefulness – it feels like the hub of the universe. It is a beautiful place.

I have the ideal clientele – four coaching clients who are paying me $1 million a year each, with a waiting list of the rich and influential who want me as their adviser. I feel privileged to be in such a position.

A little further down the hill is the creation I am most proud of – my highly profitable training institute, where people are being trained to take my methods into the world. It is run for me by a team of enthusiastic trainers.

I live a completely integrated life and achieve everything I set out to do with the greatest economy and creative power. I have great fun doing this and love my work and my life as a whole. I am changing the lives of thousands and am a major influence in the world.

I enjoy total health and look and feel younger than I did ten years ago – and am much fitter than I was then.

Let me introduce myself. I am Mark Forster's Future Self. That is to say that I am the Mark Forster who inhabits the opening scenario you have just read. Neither that scenario nor I myself yet exist. I am a product of the imagination of the Mark Forster who is currently living in the Present Reality that you are about to read. But although I am imaginary, I do have a real existence because I am part of his mental landscape. And by talking to me he will find out things about himself which he would never have been able to find out without me. So we are going to be doing quite a bit of talking together in the course of this book. This may all remind you of books like *Conversations with God*. But there are some vital differences. First, I am making no pretensions or claims to be God, or a Higher Power or even Mark's Higher Self, or whatever name you like to give it. I am simply an imaginary figure. And secondly, I am going to be the one asking the questions! That is important because I don't want anyone, least of all Mark's Present Self to start thinking that I have some sort of infallible knowledge or right answers. The important thing about me is the *perspective* from which I ask the questions. Anyway, in the dialogues that follow I will be represented by the letter Q, to signify that I am the questioner.

Present Reality

It's a beautiful picture that I have painted above. But it still lies in the future. How far have I actually got towards it?

Well, I don't have a castle overlooking the sea, but I do have a pleasant office overlooking my garden. The office is well-organised most of the time. It's a nice place to work and it expresses my personality well. There are books and pictures and plants and china ornaments in a display case. It does have a sense of spaciousness even though it is quite a small room.

I am now in my sixth month since resigning from my job and making my coaching business into my full-time work. It is a step I have not regretted for a moment.

A couple of months ago I had twenty-seven clients but I have been letting these run down as I want more time for writing and planning. This of course means a considerable drop in income which worries me a lot although I am sure I am doing the right thing.

I have been working on my second book for over six months now and I am feeling increasingly stuck – in fact I've come to the conclusion that I need to start again from scratch. The delivery date is only a bit over two months away so that is a serious decision to make.

I don't at the moment have any formal associates, though I have some loose linkages with some other coaches. Nothing much has come of any of these yet.

My weight is about right (I've lost two stone since the beginning of the year) but I would like to be fitter.

I've been working with the above vision for about four months now, during which time I got my new business firmly under way, got my office organised the way I wanted it, and achieved my goal weight. Good progress so far . . . but my feeling is I am only just beginning to get to the exciting bit!

Now I will introduce myself. I am Mark's Present Self. That is to say the one who is living the Present Reality you've just read and who is currently writing this book. I don't want to say too much about myself now because it will all come out in the dialogues. At least I think it will. I hesitated there because one fact about dialoguing with a different aspect of myself is that I don't really know beforehand what the answers are going to be. So this book may turn out to be very different from the one I am envisaging now. What I am doing here is a type of self-coaching in which I am asking myself questions from the perspective of the end result. This should be interesting because one thing that is obvious when I compare the vision with the current reality is that my Future Self is a much better coach than I am! Anyway in the dialogues that follow I will be represented by the letter A, to signify that I am giving the answers.

Tuesday, 21 August – Trusting my feelings

Q Welcome, and thank you for coming to me for coaching. It made all the difference to me to have someone like myself to coach me when I was at your stage.

A *Well, I guess you must be a pretty good coach, because my vision is to become one of the best in the world!*

Q We'll see! Perhaps you'd like to bring me up to date with the reasons why you have decided to come to me for coaching.

A *Well, the first and most obvious reason is that I want to get to the vision that I have as fast and with as little hassle as possible. And I want to be able to do this in a way that I can show other people. I believe that this kind of dialoguing is a very powerful way of achieving that.*

Q OK, what else?

A *Another reason is that I have been getting a bit stuck in writing my book. There are just over two months to go to the delivery date – two months and eleven days to be exact – and I've just taken the decision to abandon everything I've written so far and start again.*

Q Wow! That's some decision. What has made you do that?

A *I've realised that I need to make the book itself an example of everything I am saying in it. In other words I will be giving principles in the book, and the readers will actually be able to follow those principles in action in the production of the book itself.*

Q That sounds fantastic. So the book itself will be an example of the principles in action?

A *That's right. And one of the most important principles is the use of this kind of dialoguing. And another is how to create a vision that really pulls one towards it. And another is how to let it happen rather than force it.*

Q Were you forcing it before?

A *Yes, it wasn't until I realised how much I was forcing it that I saw clearly that I was producing the book without using the principles I was trying to teach in it.*

Q I don't expect you are the first person to do that!

A *No, indeed not. But it explained why I was feeling so much resistance towards the writing of the book. And once I stopped resisting my feelings of resistance I was able to see that I needed to make a fresh start in a way that I wouldn't be resisting.*

Q And you don't have any resistance to doing it this way?

A *No, I love this sort of dialogue. It's a very easy way of letting my ideas flow and getting deeper into my thinking. Also, it will give the readers a much better idea of what it actually feels like to be engaged in the process of creation. Too many books on goal achieving give the impression that there's something wrong if everything isn't going smoothly all the time.*

Q So are you seeing this dialogue as being something that's going on in real time, dealing with the problems of the day, rather than just being an academic discussion about methods of goal achievement?

A *Yes, absolutely!*

Q I'm glad you said that, because I wouldn't have let you get away with it if you hadn't!

A *No, I want this book to be real, not some academic treatise. Something which the readers can relate to their own experience even if their precise circumstances are very different from mine.*

Q OK then. Let's start dealing with the real world! Tell me what you'd like to see different as a result of this session.

A *I think the biggest problem I have at the moment is just trusting the process and allowing things to happen without worrying about it. I* *know things do come up all the time, because I'm keeping a diary to remind myself of all the wonderful things that occur each day. But that doesn't stop me trying to force things a lot of the time.*

Q So if I were able to wave a magic wand and completely solve this problem for you, what would you notice being different?

A *I'd be much more relaxed, and above all I'd have a sense of space in my life.*

Q A sense of space – that's pretty important to you, huh?

A *Yes, it's just the feeling that I have time to do the things I love doing, like calling my wife to have lunch together when I feel like it, or going and doing something really weird like meditating in a church at midnight, or just taking time off to read a book or whatever without feeling that I* ought *to be doing something else.*

Q You hate the feeling that you *ought* to be doing things?

A *Yes, I want to do things when I* want *to do them. But I want to* want *to do things when it's exactly the right time to do them too. Do you follow what I'm saying?*

Q So you want to be able to trust your feelings – that they're telling you the right thing to do?

A *Yes, that's just exactly it, but so often I just feel like goofing off or wasting time. And I hate that feeling.*

Q Have there been times when you've been able to trust your feelings in the way you want to?

A *Well, I've never really been able to let go as much as I'd like to, but I do notice looking back that nearly everything significant that has happened to me in the last few years has come through following my feelings. For instance, when I go for a walk or just sit quietly I often have my best ideas. Or sitting and reading an entire book in a morning can give me a whole host of new ideas which I then have the enthusiasm to follow through. Somehow it never quite happens like that if I have some sort of 'reading programme'. I don't get that feeling of enthusiasm.*

Q **It's the feeling of enthusiasm that carries you along is it?**

A *Yes, I only get that when I let things happen. And all my best initiatives have come through getting that sort of excitement.*

Q **What are you doing that makes that sense of excitement work?**

A *I think I'm just letting it happen, as I said. But the really good part of it is that it is so effortless. I find I don't have any resistance – everything I might have been resisting for ages has gone and suddenly gets done. It's as if a different part of me has been at work that I hardly recognise.*

Q **Who do you think this different part of you is?**

A *That's a difficult question! I think it must be me of course. But it's me when I have trust in my own abilities. No, that's not quite right. It's almost that I sort of transcend my own limitations. That there is a limited part of me and a part of me that can't be bothered with limitations.*

Q **Can't be bothered?**

A *Yes, it's like that. Can't be bothered. As if they suddenly seem too petty to be worth my attention.*

Q **And when this happens, what *is* worth your attention?**

A *I think it's being able to express myself without feeling bound by my past experience. Like trying something new. Having a new way of looking at things. I can't quite put my finger on it.*

Q **You're looking at things in a new way?**

A *Yes, like all the old ways of doing things have just departed. Like they've been carted away or something.*

Q **OK, what else would you notice different once I'd waved the magic wand?**

A *Ha! I'd get where I want to go much faster.*

Q **What would be making the difference?**

A *It's the limitation thing again. I'd refuse to accept that I have limitations.*

Q What would you be doing that would let you refuse to accept limitations?

A *I'd accept that when I felt limited or resisting it is a message that I'm not quite ready to act yet.*

Q Wow! That's interesting . . . so you'd see these things as messages?

A *Yes, I think this only works if you have a clear vision. I wouldn't like to try it if I didn't because I'd just end up doing nothing. But if I know where I want to go, I can listen to the messages that my unconscious mind is giving me through my feelings. If I find I am resisting something I can say that it's my mind telling me that it's not working for me yet.*

Q OK, I'm going to break it off there for the day because we will talk again tomorrow. I just want to end by pointing out something interesting – your methods are already working with the book.

A *They are?*

Q Yes, you've written just about 2,500 words today. That's far more than you've written in any single day up to now.

A *Right . . . it's amazing what happens when you stop resisting resistance and listen to it instead!*

Wednesday, 22 August – Push Mode and Pull Mode

Q What's been better since we spoke yesterday?

A *I've got a fantastic sense of relief at having decided to start my book again, and a sense of achievement too that I managed to write so much yesterday. And I'm really looking forward to writing more today, instead of dreading it in the way that I have been up to now. I sent off the pages I wrote yesterday to my real-life coach and she loved them.*

Q Good. That's great. Why do you think I asked you that question?

A *What? The one about what's better?*

Q Yes.

A *It didn't strike me when you asked me, but I guess I would usually expect to be asked how things have been since we last spoke, not what's better.*

Q And what would have happened if I had asked that?

A *I'd have answered with both good and bad things. And I suppose that since you are my coach, I'd have come up with a problem or two for you to solve for me!*

Q So why did I ask the question I asked?

A *So that I would consolidate the gains that I'd made?*

Q Yes, and . . . ?

A *Ah, I think I get what you're after. So my mind would start putting on a positive filter instead of a negative one?*

Q Would you like to say a bit more about that?

A *Yes . . . It's pretty well established that what we give our attention to increases and what we don't give our attention to decreases. So if we give our attention to what is growing it will tend to grow more. If we* *give our attention to our problems they will tend to multiply. Hey, I've got a great idea!*

Q **Yes?**

A *I'm due to write an article today for my weekly newsletter. I haven't decided on the subject yet, so why don't I write it on what we've just been talking about and then I can put it in the book as well? Kill two birds with one stone!*

Q **Brilliant idea. Go ahead!**

From problem solving to growth – How to make the change

It's a well-known fact that what we give our attention to grows and what we don't give our attention to tends to fade away.

The trouble is often that what we give our attention to is our problems. Sometimes our lives get to the stage when they seem to be one long list of problems to solve. And when we get more problems than we think we are ever going to be capable of solving, we get into a state of overwhelm. And being in a state of overwhelm is yet another bigger and better problem that needs solving!

What is the average 'To Do' list but a list of problems that we have tasked ourselves with fixing?

- Clear e-mail backlog.
- Sort out desk.
- Find the file on Project A.
- Catch up with accounts.
- Ring irate customer.
- Look at why sales are falling.
- Find out why X sent that stupid letter.
- Make a workable policy for incoming enquiries.
- Get Project B back on track.

- Read a book on time management!
- etc. etc.

Most of the creative, enjoyable things rarely feature on 'To Do' lists. They are kept for 'when I have enough time'. And of course there never is enough time because our lives contain a potentially infinite number of problems. Have you ever noticed how a 'To Do' list has a tendency to grow? Because for every one problem we strike off the top of the list, we think up another three or four problems to write on its end.

The only way out of this is a complete change in attitude. We need to get our eyes off our problems and onto the good things in our lives. Or even better, get our eyes onto what is growing in our lives.

So let's stop asking ourselves, 'What are the problems in my life that I need to fix?' A good question to ask instead is, 'What are the good things that happened today?'

An even better question is, 'What was better about today?' If we ask ourselves that question, we are focusing our attention on the areas in our lives in which there is growth and forward movement. And once we have focused our minds on those areas, our minds will want more and will actively go searching for it.

I asked myself that question last night, and here are some of the answers:

- Helped my daughter with her course work without either of us getting annoyed (major breakthrough!).
- Wrote 2,500 words of dialogue for my book.
- Did what I liked when I felt like it and the world didn't fall to pieces.
- Weight firmly back within acceptable limits.
- Completed a chapter of my Spanish textbook.
- Got to bed on time for the third night running.
- Had a brilliant idea for a new seminar.
- Got confirmation of some potential seminars.
- Decided to go on a course in the USA in October.

I could have produced a magnificent list of problems to be solved had I wanted to and thoroughly depressing they would have been too. But instead I have firmly marked yesterday down as a success and I feel enthusiastic about getting yet more successes because they make me feel good. No, not good – they make me feel *better!*

Exercise
At the end of the day, sit down briefly with a sheet of paper (or your computer) and ask yourself the question, 'What was better about today?' Write down as many things as you can think of. It doesn't matter how big or small they are. They can range from, 'I managed to fry an egg without breaking the yolk' up to, 'Today I found the partner of my dreams,' and beyond. Daily practice of this exercise will help to change you from a problem-centred focus to a growth-centred focus.

Q That's great. What was significant for you about doing that?

A *Hmmm . . . the really interesting thing for me about all this is that both writing my book and getting my newsletter out are flowing out of this dialogue.*

Q You were resisting getting your newsletter out as well?

A *Yes, it's always a major struggle. The writing is easy but getting started is the problem. Anyway this time I had decided to leave it until I felt ready to write it, and lo and behold! it's written – and I hardly noticed it happening!*

Q Fantastic. So that will go onto your 'What's better about today?' list, will it?

A *You bet! I've already put it on.*

Q You look as if you want to ask me something.

A *Yes, I want to ask you if you are still writing a daily 'What's Better?' list way off in the future?*

Q What do you think?

A *Yes, I think you are. From what I know of you, you are completely growth-orientated and I guess this is a very effective way of maintaining that attitude. Also something just struck me that I hadn't thought of before . . .*

Q Yes?

A *Well, you live in* my *Future Vision. But it's just occurred to me that you will have your* own *Future Vision and therefore your own Future Self. So I would be interested to know whether you are being coached by* him.

Q All you are really saying is that you will keep expanding your vision as you progress and you will still be using the same methods to achieve it.

A *Yes, sometimes I do tend to forget that you are just me imagining me in the future! Still someday it might be a good mind-expanding exercise to ask you what your vision for your future is.*

Q It would. But let's leave that for the end of the book, shall we?

A *OK.*

Q Now I want to go back to the messages that resistance has for you. We've dealt with two major areas – writing your book and writing your newsletter. What else are you resisting in your life at the moment?

A *Ugh! I hate that question . . . I suppose getting my website finished is the major one. I've been putting that off for months. Every time I take some action towards it, I seem to pull back deliberately from the point of actually completing it.*

Q OK, so if that resistance were a powerful message from your mind to you, what would it be saying?

A *I guess it would have to be saying that I don't want a website, or at least that I don't want* that *website. Or it might be saying that I'm not ready for a website* yet. *I think I've always tended to feel that a website is something that I* ought *to have.*

Q So you don't have a real vision for your website at the moment?

A *I think I don't have a vision that I'm entirely happy with. And I think another problem is that having a website would actually commit me to things I don't necessarily want to be committed to. In other words I would have to define who I am and what I am offering at a time when I'm still exploring these myself. Also I would have to produce a programme of seminars and other attractions. So it's not just the website – it's what goes with it. And there again what is the point of it at the moment? I don't actually want too many clients right now. I want to have time to get my book finished and to develop what it is that I intend to be doing in the future.*

Q Those all sound like good reasons to me. So in spite of them all, you've been trying to force yourself to get the website finished just because you feel you *ought* to?

A *Er, yes, I guess so! I suppose I should know by now that my feelings are usually right.*

Q Or at the least worth taking seriously?

A *Yes, when I find myself resisting something I can be pretty sure it's my mind giving me a red light or possibly an amber one.*

Q And what's it like when your mind gives a *green* light to something?

A *It just sort of happens. It's as if I want to do it, and know I have the oomph to do it as well.*

Q So when your mind gives you a green light, you get the power you need as well?

A *Yes, I hadn't thought of it quite that way before.*

Q Now I want to ask you what I hope won't be too embarrassing a question. In your previous book *Get Everything Done and Still Have Time to Play* you talked about something you called the resistance principle. I think you said something on the lines of resistance being a signpost to where you should be going. How does that square with what you are saying now?

A *Yes, that's a very good question. I said that if you aim to do what you are resisting the most first you will virtually automatically do the right thing at the right time, because resistance is a sign that you are going out of your comfort zone. And getting out of your comfort zone is where you need to be if you are going to develop and grow.*

Q OK, so have you changed your mind on that?

A *I don't think I've changed my mind so much as gone beyond it. What I wrote about resistance in my book is great for people who are working in what I call Push Mode.*

Q What do you mean by that?

A *It's the opposite of what I call Pull Mode. Essentially the difference is that in Push Mode you are pushing yourself towards your goals. In Pull Mode you are allowing your goals to pull you towards them. The results may look much the same, but Pull Mode is much less effortful and relies more on the unconscious activity of the brain rather than conscious linear processing. Perhaps it would make it clearer if I inserted a table here showing some of the differences.*

Push Mode	Pull Mode
Pushing oneself towards one's goals	Allowing goals to pull one towards them
Emphasis on conscious linear thought	Emphasis on holistic unconscious processing
Relatively effortful	Relatively effortless

Push Mode *continued*	Pull Mode *continued*
Emphasis on planning	Emphasis on letting opportunities arise
Concrete, measurable, discrete goals	Narrative, descriptive, overall vision
When progress is slow, improve the plans	When progress is slow, improve the vision
Obstacles are enemies	Obstacles are friends
Resistance seen as an obstacle to be overcome	Resistance seen as a message to be listened to
Making things happen	Letting things happen
Motivated by outside pressures	Motivated by inner feelings

Q So are you saying that your first book was mainly about Push Mode?

A *Yes, and since the majority of people are in Push Mode it gives a lot of very useful techniques for them. But my aim in the book we are writing now is to describe how to move into a whole new way of living. And when we succeed in moving into Pull Mode, we are relying on the mind's unconscious processing so we have to be much more alert to the signals it gives.*

Q Can we use this when we are still in Push Mode?

A *It could be very dangerous to do so. Because the essence of Pull Mode is to have a vision that is so strong that it pulls one towards it. If you don't have a vision that strong, your mind is not going to be giving you clear signals. That's basically why 'letting it happen' is such a disaster for most people – because they haven't put the structure in place beforehand which targets the mind. Without that sort of clear vision most people are better off in Push Mode.*

Q Hmmm . . . so just what *are* you going to do about your website?

A *Aaargh . . . you certainly know how to bring me back to earth! Well, I need to apply my own principles. I have a strong vision for the future so I should be able to trust my mind to produce a green light at the exact right time for having a website. And until then I should stop worrying about it.*

Q Good! It's nice to know that you intend to walk your talk . . . Going on, I think it would be good for us to discuss how to produce this strong vision that you have been talking about. Perhaps we could do that tomorrow?

A *Yes, but before we do that I think it would be a good idea for me to summarise where we have got to, don't you?*

Q I do. But let's leave all that to tomorrow. And, guess what, we've written another 2,500 words today!

A *There's no guessing about it. I have been very conscious of it. And I have been determined all along to be able to put this second day's success on my 'What's Better?' list for today.*

Q Which just shows the power of writing that list every day!

Thursday, 23 August – Writing powerful goals

Q So what's been better since we spoke yesterday?

A *Well, I had a really amazing validation of how important it is to follow one's feelings and not to do things just because you feel you ought to.*

Q Yes?

A *As you know I left my employment at the end of February and within a couple of months I had as many clients as I could handle. So I was already earning quite a bit more than I had been in my job.*

Q I remember how amazed you were at how well it had worked out . . . and so quickly too.

A *Yes, I thought it would take me at least a year to build the coaching practice up. But over the last couple of months I started getting a strong feeling that I should not be trying to replace clients once they finished since I wanted more time to write and to concentrate on fulfilling my overall vision.*

Q Which only has four coaching clients in it if I remember right?

A *You tell me! You're the one who lives there. But anyway it was quite a scary decision to make. Here I was having built up a successful practice now proposing to demolish it and take a new direction – all within the space of a few months.*

Q So what's happened to validate this decision?

A *Well, I've just this morning landed five days' work in September giving seminars at a major household name company. It will pay much more than the missing clients, and if I'd still had as many clients I wouldn't have been able to fit it in.*

Q And how did you succeed in landing this work?

A *Well, I'll tell you one thing, I didn't get it by planning to get it. It just came to me.*

Q So you just sat back and let it come to you?

A *No, it came to me because all the things I have done in the past through following my feelings and instincts attracted it. There was no sitting back involved!*

Q Ah! That sounds like an important point. It seems you've done an incredible job of living your own principles here.

A *Well, I wouldn't say that exactly because I am conscious of how often I get into Push Mode. But what I have become very aware of is that it is what I do when I am in Pull Mode that produces the real results. The Push Mode stuff seems very sterile by comparison.*

Q So am I right in thinking that you want to be living more purely in Pull Mode?

A *Yes, that is just exactly what this book is all about. How to live in Pull Mode to the greatest possible extent.*

Q What are the times when you find it easiest to live in Pull Mode?

A *That's a good question because Pull Mode is very difficult for most people, including myself, to live in – at least initially. I know that I have a problem myself because it involves letting go of the conscious planning parts of myself and surrendering to the more unconscious feeling parts of myself. And in the initial stages that can be very messy.*

Q How do you mean 'messy'?

A *Well, literally messy. I've written a book and given seminars on how to keep one's work up to date and be totally on top of one's e-mails and paperwork, etc. etc. and yet here I am letting go of all that and only doing my e-mails and paperwork and all the rest when I feel like it. Which isn't always that often!*

Q Well at least you are not allowing yourself to get trapped by your own message!

A *That's a very real problem with many people who have written books. They get trapped by their own message and can't let go of it so that they can go on beyond it.*

Q You used the word 'initially'. Are you saying that this messy state is only temporary?

A *Well, I hope it is! If you go back to my vision at the beginning of the book, you'll notice that it includes a sense of spaciousness and is obviously very well ordered. So being well ordered is one aspect of the vision that is pulling me towards it. So my guess is that as I allow myself to get more and more into Pull Mode, so orderliness will happen naturally.*

Q And in the meantime . . . ?

A *I am living with a bit of a messy desk!*

Q OK, can we get back to the question I originally asked, which is what are the times you find it easiest to live in Pull Mode?

A *That's easy to answer. It's easiest to live like that when I have a very definite green light in my mind about something. In other words I get a strong impulse to do something and the energy to do it just comes bubbling up.*

Q What's different about those times?

A *I guess I just sort of stop worrying about what I* ought *to be doing. I let go of it and just have faith in the process. If it needs to be done, it'll get done in its own time and if it doesn't need to be done, it won't.*

Q That sounds very New Age-y to me!

A *Well I think the New Age style is a reaction to the constant push, push, push of most of the modern world. But the problem is that there is a third state, which is that instead of pushing or being pulled you can just be drifting. And a lot of the New Age stuff sometimes seems to be more about drifting than it is about being pulled. That's an enormous generalisation of course.*

Q And you are not keen on drifting?

A *The trouble with drifting is that there is a big tendency to lose touch with reality. And losing touch with reality causes a huge amount of generalised anxiety. Which in its turn tends to be palliated by such things as drug abuse and so on.*

Q So being in Pull Mode is quite different from drifting?

A *Yes, and the essential difference is that in Pull Mode you have a strong vision, which is pulling you.*

Q Right! Sounds like we've got back to where we left off last night. How do we get this vision?

A *Before we talk about that, I'd like to summarise where we have got to so far.*

Q OK, but before you do that I'd like to give you a challenge.

A *OK?*

Q I'd like you to find one thing each day to put on your 'What's Better?' list specifically on the subject of being well ordered.

A *Right! Er . . . what happens if I can't find anything?*

Q You can *always* find something that's better, even if it's something that seems totally trivial.

A *If you say so . . . Now let's do this summary!*

Summary – The three modes of living

- There are three modes of living:
  1. Push Mode
  2. Drift Mode
  3. Pull Mode
- Most people in the everyday world of work are in Push Mode. This is basically characterised by *making* things happen.

- Some people try to escape from the stresses of Push Mode by drifting. This is characterised by aimlessness.
- Relatively few people manage to live to a greater or lesser extent in Pull Mode. This is characterised by *letting* things happen.
- Pull Mode bears some superficial resemblances to drifting in that one only does what one feels like doing, but the essential difference is that Pull Mode has a strong vision as the motivating force.
- Pull Mode also has some superficial resemblances to Push Mode in that it is highly productive, but the essential difference is that the high productivity is achieved effortlessly (which doesn't mean without any work).
- Pull Mode uses the mind's powerful unconscious processing. This can be enhanced by use of such methods as:
  1. A strong vision.
  2. Using the imagination to interact with that vision by dialoguing with your 'Future Self'.
  3. Concentrating on the growth areas of one's life by means of a daily 'What's Better?' list.
- As far as moment-by-moment action is concerned, the mind will normally signal what to do by means of strong impulse as a green light, and resistance as an amber or red light.
- What this boils down to is that you should do whatever you feel like doing at the time. But note that this only works if you actually *are* in Pull Mode. Otherwise you are going to find yourself drifting.

Q That seems very clear to me. But there is one very important ingredient which we haven't discussed yet. And that is how do we get that powerful vision in the first place?

A *Right. There are two elements involved in getting a vision which will pull you towards it. You can see both of these in my vision at the beginning of this book. First of all I gave the vision itself. That was where you introduced yourself.*

Q I remember!

A *And then you need the Present Reality – that's where I introduced myself. The mind wants to resolve the difference between the two. That is what creates the force that pulls you towards the goal.*

Q So if you want to get somewhere you need to know where you are now?

A *Yes, because if you don't you are what is known as 'lost'!*

Q And that applies just as much to arriving at goals as to map reading, does it?

A *Yes, we see it all around us. People refusing to face up to the Present Reality of where they are. How many firms have gone bust because of it? How many people have stayed stuck in dead-end jobs? How many relationships have been destroyed?*

Q You're obviously very concerned by this.

A *Yes, it's extremely important. In fact when working with my clients often the real breakthroughs have been made when they have faced up to Present Reality, rather than when they've constructed a vision for themselves.*

Q So how does this relationship between Present Reality and the vision actually work in practice?

A *I think I'd like to show you an e-mail one of my clients sent me, which gives a real-life example of how this can work on a short-term goal. I have her permission to quote it.*

Rebecca's testimony

I started writing down my vision about a month before an important gig at which my manager – who had so far only heard my demo – was going to hear me for the first time.

I was very thorough, mentioning specific songs etc, although I changed things along the way. I wrote about the band, how they and the audience would react to me, how my manager would feel about me, how I would look, what I would wear, how I would do my hair.

One thing it really did was take away all the usual indecisiveness I have about what to wear and stuff. It also got me honing my set list practically from the day I began writing my vision, as opposed to the day before the gig. I found it was actually *much* more effective to be prepared, which kind of surprised me because it is jazz music and about feeling the moment so it seemed odd to plan ahead. However, I realise that when you know a song really, really well that is when you can truly do your best job on improvising on the changes on the spur of the moment. I think it was like that.

At the beginning my Present Reality was all, 'Oh I am crap, who do I think I am, I feel shitty,' but gradually as the weeks progressed my vision stayed more or less the same but my Present Reality turned into 'Did my vocal exercises every day, worked on my set list, perfected my accent on this Portuguese . . . whatever.'

On the actual day, much of my vision came true. The sound system was not great and I could not hear myself very well and, in a few of the early songs in the first set, the arrangements did not go according to plan. However, overall, the band chemistry was amazing – especially given that we didn't rehearse at all. The guys played so brilliantly all of them. My own song was so well received that other singers asked who wrote it, and when I said 'Me' one said she would like to do it. Also my lyrics to instrumentals.

My manager *did* love me despite the errors and she and the pianist discussed (she told me later) the fact that I had this thing called 'it' and another thing called 'the x-factor'. So I would say that it was pretty successful.

The room *was* packed (so many people came that some of them were sent away and told to come back for the second set), the audience *were* appreciative, I made *more* on the door than I asked for. The guys really enjoyed playing together and with me, they want to work with me regularly, the drummer was clapping at the end of my ballads even, I felt totally respected by them, I looked fabulous (so everyone said), my manager was extremely happy. I must say it was also rather thrilling to have her there and be seen by all the singers who had also tried to get her and failed to. I guess that is a bit mean of me – or is it so bad? Maybe it's only like that feeling of winning a race.

So now *onward*. I am continuing to do my vision. When I don't have specific dates to work towards I concentrate on a longer-term vision. I really recommend it. I feel as focused on my musical career and my music as an athlete at a game. I am a laser beam *honed* in to my musical career. I write songs, compose lyrics, do vocal exercises, plan arrangements, learn new songs. As I write about being asked by musicians to do gigs, amazingly I *do* get asked. By random strangers even. Very weird. It is as if I am conjuring these things up.

Q That's pretty impressive. So what was she doing that made the difference to how she was before?

A *I think this is the cue to get another document out of the archives. I want to show you the instructions that I gave to her (and all my clients) on how to do this vision work.*

Q That would be really interesting. And guess what? We've just done another 2,500 words today.

A *That's amazing! Three days in a row. And the document will take us way over that total. That's really something for the 'What's Better?' list!*

The Goal Achievement Method

There are considerable problems with most of the methods of setting goals and targets that we are commonly taught. Admittedly any goals are better than no goals, but most of us have experienced the uncomfortable fact that just because we have set ourselves a goal we aren't necessarily going to achieve it.

Generally, the problem with the traditional methods of goal setting is that they encourage us to use our rational minds but ignore deeper levels of mental processing. They also ignore the fact that it is our feelings that are the primary motivators in our lives. If our feelings are at odds with our goals we will almost inevitably find some way of sabotaging our own efforts. It is no use setting goals which do not relate to us as complete human beings.

If we are going to set goals that really motivate us we must present them in such a way that we succeed in selling them to ourselves. And every salesperson knows that what the customer buys is an image rather than reality. So we need to sell our goals in the same way – this time to ourselves.

What we want v. What we don't want

Strangely enough one of the biggest problems that many people have when they first start to set significant goals for their lives is that they have great difficulty identifying what they want. Most of us are so hemmed in by the expectations of other people and the various *musts*, *shoulds* and *oughts* that we have accumulated that the idea of writing down what we really want can be quite anxiety-making or guilt-making. I have had clients who have initially been completely unable to identify anything that they want purely for themselves; and others who have denied that it is possible to get anything that they really want. The trouble is, that however deeply they suppress what they do want they will continue to sabotage the things that they don't really want. This may result in a person getting the worst of both worlds – neither getting what they want nor satisfying their need for the approval of others.

Often the best way to identify what you really *do* want is to start with what you *don't* want and then consider what the positive opposite of that would be.

Exercise 1

Divide a sheet of paper into two columns and in the left-hand column write a list of everything you can think of that you don't want to *be*, e.g. unhappy, lonely, fat, disorganised, unemployed, ill, broke, etc. etc. Then in the right-hand column write your positive opposite of each item, e.g. happy, popular, slim, organised, productive, healthy, wealthy, etc. It doesn't matter whether the word is the exact dictionary opposite or not – the important thing is that it represents the opposite for you. You can then write this out again: 'I want to be happy, popular, slim, etc.' Congratulations! You have just identified some of the things you really want to be.

Exercise 2

Now repeat the last exercise, but this time write down everything you don't want to *have* in your life. This can range from the wrong job or an abusive spouse to an untidy desk or a cracked window. Next, as before, write the positive opposite of each item. Congratulations again! You have just discovered some of the things you really want to have.

Exercise 3

Now that you have loosened up a bit by working from what you don't want, it's time to have a go at working directly at what you do want.

Take a blank sheet of paper and head it 'I would like . . .' Then write a list of every single thing you can think of that you would really like to have or to do or to be. Imagine that you have no constraints. Don't worry about possibility or morality or consequences (for yourself or for others). Just get it all out onto paper. You are not saying that you are going to have these things, just that you'd like to have them. This is an exercise to enjoy. So really let your imagination go!

Now go through the list and see if you can find one item in it which you could actually have *now, right this minute* if you decided to. What's stopping you? Go ahead!

Now for each item on the list, ask yourself, 'If I could actually have this in real life would I really want it?' If the answer is 'No' to any item, cross it off the list. Re-read the list again and then put it away so that you can refer to it later.

Feelings

I mentioned that the real motivators in our lives are our feelings. We can take advantage of this to help us to get where we want to go in our lives. If we can describe things in terms of how we feel about them – particularly in terms of how we will feel when we have them – then we will be starting the process of activating the filtering mechanism of our minds to home in on the target.

This ability of our brains to filter our experience is quite extraordinary. A good example of this is what happens when we buy a new car. Suddenly we become aware of all the cars of the same colour and model that pass us. We don't have to consciously watch out for them – our brains automatically present them to our conscious awareness. In the same way, once we have latched onto something we really want, our minds continuously present us with opportunities that will take us in the right direction. The opportunities were there all along – just as the cars were in our example – but it is only when our minds are really engaged that we notice them.

Exercise 4

Take your want list from Exercise 3 and chose one item from it – go for the one that stands out for you the most as you look down the list. Now visualise what it would be like if you achieved it. Try and imagine the moment you reach it for the first time. Write a few sentences to describe that moment. How would you feel? What emotions would be going through your mind? Make your description as vivid as possible.

When you have finished writing it, re-read it and this time imagine it to be an advertisement. Have you succeeded in selling it to yourself? If not, how could you make it more enticing?

Writing

Research has shown that people who have set themselves long-term goals are much more likely to be successful in life than those who have not – it has also shown that those who have written goals are much more likely to be successful than those who have kept their goals solely in their minds.

And even more successful – the most successful of the successful of the successful as it were – are those who regularly write out their goals so that they are imprinted on their minds. One of the most fundamental parts of my goal-setting method is the regular writing out of goals. But this brings another advantage too. Let's now look at what this is.

When we take an action such as writing about a problem our brains continue to process it subconsciously after we have finished. The result is that if we come back to a piece of written work after an interval of time we find that our thinking has moved on. It is as if putting the problem on paper enables the mind to integrate where it has got to, which then allows it to take a further leap forward.

So one of the most essential parts of the method is to revise what we have written regularly. To start with, this is probably best done on a daily basis but we can lengthen the interval once the goal has got well established in our minds. To see how this works try the following exercise.

Exercise 5

To see how the mind continues to process after we have finished consciously thinking about something, try repeating a simple sentence completion exercise at intervals.

Let's pick one that might be useful to you. Write as many endings as you can think of to the following sentence beginning:

'Something I could do which might improve my life right now is . . .'

> The secret when writing endings to sentences like this is to write them as quickly as possible off the top of your head without pausing for thought. There is no need for the endings to make sense, least of all to be 'sensible'. Nor do you have to commit to doing any of the things you write down.

Come back to this exercise after an interval of a few hours and re-do it without looking at your previous workings. You will almost certainly find that your thoughts have moved on and you have quite a bit of new material. In fact you can repeat this several times and come up with new ideas each time.

The significance of this for our purpose is that revising our goals and vision on a regular basis is a very good way of refining them and of ensuring that they are indeed what we really want. It is perfectly possible that writing a goal out on a daily basis may bring us to the realisation that we don't really want it at all. This is not a failure of the system but a success. The realisation that we don't really want something can save us from some horrendous mistakes or at the very least from wasting time we could have put to better use.

So to sum up, the way to set and refine a goal in such away that it will target our mind is to make use of the four elements of:

- Feelings
- Writing
- Repetition
- Revision

However, setting a goal is only the first step in getting our minds to take us where we want to be. Knowing our destination is essential of course, but if we are going to get to our destination we also need to know where we are starting from. So the second element in the method is to examine our Present Reality with respect to the goal.

Present Reality

It is not just the feelings that we *will* have when we achieve our goal that motivate us towards it. Just as important are the feelings that we *do* have about our present situation with regard to it. So once we have written out the goal, the second step is to write out exactly where we are in relation to the goal, both in terms of facts and our feelings about those facts. It is very important not to deny the negative when we do this. The biggest danger of so-called positive thinking is that it can cut us off from our true feelings – and unacknowledged feelings have far more power over us than ones that have been acknowledged and accepted.

So to summarise, what you need in order to target your mind is a clear idea of where you are going and an equally clear picture of where you are. Both of these need to be regularly updated.

Exercise 6

To get proficiency in making this method work it is best not to start off by using it on something long, difficult and complicated. Start by using it on easy things first until you are comfortable with it. For your first attempt I suggest that you pick something that doesn't *have* to be done by a particular date, but *could* be completed in less than a day. I will use the example of clearing an e-mail backlog.

First decide what the goal is:

I want to clear my backlog of e-mail.

How does the idea of clearing a backlog of e-mail make you feel? If you are like most people the answer is that it feels pretty depressing! Clearing a backlog is an example of describing what you *don't* want (a backlog) rather than what you *do* want. So rephrase the goal so that it describes what you do want:

I want to be completely up to date with my e-mail.

How does that make you feel? Any better?

If you are trying to work out how to do something an effective technique is to imagine that you have achieved it and then describe how you did it. In the same way we can increase the power of our goal by imagining what it will be like when we have got there. So put the goal in the present tense as if you were describing it once you have reached it:

I am completely up to date with my e-mail.

Now add feelings!

I am delighted that I am completely up to date with my e-mail. It's taken a load off my mind.

Now check that the emotions are ones which you do want, not ones which you don't want. The key is to examine what words you are using. Here you have used the word 'load', which is definitely a don't want! So rephrase it to include the positive opposite of 'load' – perhaps words like 'light', 'easy' or 'relaxed'.

I am delighted that I am completely up to date with my e-mail. My work is so much easier now and I feel much more relaxed.

That's your goal drafted. Now write the facts about the present situation:

I have a backlog of 400 e-mails, some of which may require urgent attention. I am currently receiving about 30 e-mails a day.

Add your present feelings:

I have a backlog of 400 e-mails, I've been resisting looking at them and I have a horrible feeling that some of them may be important. The whole thing is like a black cloud hovering over me. And every day I get at least another 30. I feel overwhelmed by the volume and hopeless that I will ever be able to control them.

The final step is to revise this at regular intervals, preferably daily to start off with (with a small goal of course you may have completed it in less than a day). If you keep your goal on your word processor, read the goal through carefully and change any of it that you want to. You might want to make it stronger, or get rid of some negative bits ('don't wants'), or you might have come to a clearer picture of what exactly it is that you do want. Then underneath the goal write out your current reality fresh each time, paying particular attention to your feelings.

One thing I have discovered from keeping a diary of my feelings in this way is how cyclical my feelings are. This has helped me to realise that it is inevitable that I will have times when I am feeling discouraged – but if I keep going the feelings will not last for long.

Often it is in honestly exploring and describing one's feelings in the Present Reality that the real breakthroughs are made. Here is an example of just such a breakthrough.

Matthew's testimony

Just thought I'd give some feedback on your method. My goal is to complete and hand in my psychology research project by 7 May. I have done the writing exercise for the first eight days, had a two-day break, done two days more, had one day's break and now have been doing it for the last three days. Initially my writing in step one was quite general, i.e. *I have handed in two copies of my research project spiral bound in blue.* Increasingly I have started to put a little more detail about what the project contains (which is the hard part), i.e. *It contains a detailed and thorough analysis of the discursive functions of football commentators' talk.*

I must say that for a while there I felt like stopping using the method as I felt that I was not getting anywhere. It was as though I was treading water – however, yesterday came a major breakthrough. It came after I admitted to myself that I was completely bored with the project, that I had picked the worst possible project and methodology, that I hated the project and that I didn't want to do it.

I then asked myself why I was doing it, and the answer was that I wanted to finish my degree and get the qualification that I'd spent the last five years pursuing.

I then said, 'What do I need to do?' and the answer was 'Get 35%'. I then began to wonder what a 35% project would look like. I imagined it would be strung together – it would have all the relevant sections and would be vaguely on the mark. I then looked at the work I had already done and saw that I could probably string the entire thing together from what I had already done and hand it in.

As I began to do this I started speeding up. I then began work on the analysis (which is the hard part). Without realising it I had made a major perceptual shift – the one needed to do this kind of analysis and my analysis was flowing really well. At the end of the night I had realised that I was no longer just looking at passing – I was now glimpsing the possibility of a really high mark!

Friday, 24 August – The trouble with linear thinking

Q What's been better since we last spoke?

A *You asked me to find something to put on the 'What's Better?' list about being well ordered.*

Q Yes, I did.

A *The only thing I could find was that I made all my phone calls during the day immediately.*

Q That's great! What were you doing that allowed you to get those done?

A *I don't really know. I think I just sort of leapt in rather than put them off.*

Q And what effect has putting that on the day's 'What's Better?' list had on you?

A *I don't know how it works but somehow it makes me feel that I'm going to be answering phone calls immediately from now on. And in fact now I think of it, I already did that this morning. I got a letter from my publisher and rang straight back to answer the point they raised.*

Q Fantastic! And were there other times during the day when you were well ordered?

A *Oh, yes. I don't want to give the impression that I am living in total disorder at the moment. I got everything done that needed doing quickly.*

Q Good, so you could put that on your list too?

A *Yes, I suppose I could!*

Q Don't forget to find something every day to go on the list about being well ordered.

A *OK.*

Q So what's your general feeling about how you are doing at the moment?

A *Well, a couple of weeks ago I was really feeling quite discouraged. I was getting stuck on my book. I had been trying out various new time management techniques that didn't work for very long. I had taken the decision to let my client numbers run down but I was very worried about what that would do to my income.*

Q And now?

A *All those things seem to have resolved themselves. I made the decision to scrap what I'd done on my book and start again using the principles we've been discussing. And that in itself has validated the principles to me in a new way and made me have much more faith in them. The worries about income have been resolved. But above all I have an incredible feeling of confidence now.*

Q All in three days?

A *In a way. It was the decision to write the book in this way that really seems to have made the difference. Because what I realise happened was that for the first time I was applying the principles to every area of my life.*

Q And what effect did that have?

A *It was like suddenly getting a much tighter control. Up to now, yes, I've been using the principles of 'pull' rather than 'push' but it's been rather a hit-and-miss process. I've achieved a lot through using them. I was able to give up my job, go full time into my coaching business and be earning more after only two months than I was before. That was a tremendous vindication to me of what I believed in. But I still didn't feel I was really making the most out of the principles.*

Q And now you do?

A *Yes, I feel that it's all come together at last.*

Q And how likely do you think you are to be able to maintain this?

A *Well, I don't think that I am never going to get discouraged again. But I am pretty confident that I now have a workable system of consistently living in Pull Mode. And this means that I will be able to move forward faster and more efficiently. There won't be so much friction in my life. I think what I really mean is faster and more effortlessly, rather than efficiently.*

Q You've used the word 'effortlessly' before. What are you doing when life is moving forward effortlessly?

A *I think it's what is often called 'working in the flow'. It's when you are so absorbed in a task that it almost seems to do itself. It's a great feeling because you are actually using all your abilities in the most effective way. So you feel that everything in you is involved in what you are doing.*

Q So when you say that you are achieving things effortlessly, you don't mean without doing any work?

A *No, quite definitely not. I've put a lot of hard work into my business. But it's not been a case of having to push myself to do it. Actually that's not quite true, because there have been plenty of times when I haven't lived up to my principles and* have *tried to push myself. But the interesting thing is that those have been the times which haven't really borne any fruit. So not only did I expend a great deal of unnecessary effort in trying to push myself, but also I didn't get anything out of it . . . Apart from a very valuable lesson of course! . . . I'd like to tell you the story of how I started off in my new business, which illustrates the point very well.*

Q OK. I'm listening!

Setting up a new business – Mark's story

Giving up the security of a salary is never an easy thing, but I had got to the point where I knew it was now or never if I was ever going to start up my own business. I had written a book which had received good publicity. I was getting a good number of enquiries for coaching clients and also I had succeeded in paying off all my debts, including my mortgage, so we could survive on a minimum of money. There could never be a better time so finally I decided to take the plunge.

I started planning how I was going to build my business up. And in order to do that I used the method which in one form or another is found in many management and business planning books. I first of all set myself goals for three years' time, then worked back to where I wanted to be in one year's time, then in six months' time, then in a month's time, then a week's time, and finally wrote down everything I needed to do that day.

I remember looking at that bit of paper which contained I don't know how many items with a sense of complete horror. I realised that I had just condemned myself to a three-year sentence of ticking items off a never-ending succession of lists of things to do. Was this what running my own business meant? A sense of deadness and paralysis started to envelop me. I just felt tired of the whole thing – and I hadn't even started to do anything yet!

This wonderful plan covered about six sheets of paper and had taken me several hours to complete. With a sense of incredible relief I tore the whole thing up and threw it into the waste paper basket.

I never missed it for a second.

I have no idea what my business would be like today if I had forced myself to put that plan into effect. But I am quite sure that I would not have enjoyed it one tiny bit as much as I actually have. And as I've said already, it only took me two months to be earning more than I was before.

Q That is very interesting. But are there times when planning is necessary?

A *Yes, I've got nothing against planning as such, any more than I have against rational conscious thought. But they need to be seen as specific precision tools to be used where appropriate, rather than the main or even sole method of operating.*

Q And what do you see as the main method of operating?

A *The whole idea behind what I am saying is to enable us to* let *things happen rather than* make *them happen. This means that we will be using the unconscious areas of our minds. I am not saying anything magical or mystical here. The role of unconscious mental processing is well established experimentally. A good book on the subject is* Hare Brain, Tortoise Mind *by Guy Claxton. A couple of sentences from it will illustrate what I mean:*

> *. . . it is not that in uncertain conditions we have to 'make do' with intuition, as if we were clutching at straws. It is that well-developed, tentatively used intuition is actually the best tool for the job; while the apparent solidity of a rational, strategic plan offers nothing more than a comforting illusion.*

Q 'A comforting illusion', that's good!

A *He then goes on to quote Henry Mintzberg, professor of management at McGill University, in* The Rise and Fall of Strategic Planning:

> *A good deal of corporate planning . . . is like a ritual rain-dance. It has no effect on the weather that follows, but those who engage in it think it does . . . Moreover, much of the advice related to corporate planning is directed at improving the dancing, not the weather.*

Q I like that!

A *I've certainly found it rings bells in my own experience.*

Q But to go back to my earlier question, what are the times when planning *is* necessary?

A *Well, I'd like to expand on this at a bit more length, and it's also got big implications for how we look at problems.*

Q ***Problems*****? Are you telling me that people who use your methods are still going to have** ***problems*****?**

A *Ha, ha! Very funny! Yes, of course they are, but it's the way they look at their problems that makes all the difference.*

Problems

Books about achieving goals seem to be divided into two camps. There are those that advocate a very linear approach to setting goals. You are advised to set yourself clearly defined goals at various points in time. So you might for instance do what I tried to do when I started planning my business – start out by setting goals for achievement in five years' time. Then you would work back from these by setting goals for three years' time, one year's time, one month, one week and finally goals for action today. The majority of business management books advocate this approach or some sort of variation of it. If you are trying to build a motorway, or organise the next Olympic games, this sort of approach, or something like it, is very useful, indeed essential. But the trouble is that what is a specific tool designed for specific situations doesn't work very well when it is applied to life in general. I remember when I was young my father, a civil servant, spent a great deal of time working on something called the National Plan. It was finally published to great fanfares in the press. Britain now had an integrated economic plan that would lead it out of the wilderness. Within a matter of weeks along came the National Dock Strike and the National Plan was never heard of again.

The trouble with the linear approach to goals is that it essentially sees life as a series of problems that need to be overcome. So it works fine when it is dealing with a specific project in which the problems are relatively easy to define and isolate. But when we are dealing with the whole of life this adversarial approach to problems has severe limitations.

The second type of goal-setting book is more likely to be found on the self-help or body-mind-spirit sections of your bookshop rather than the business and management sections. In these books the emphasis is placed on *asking* for the goal. The way this is done varies but invariably involves some sort of higher power which may be described as God, the Universe, one's Higher Self, the Unconscious Mind, etc. Essentially the idea is that the request is handed over to this higher power and the role of the asker is then to wait in faith for the higher power to grant the request.

Now I have a healthy respect for God, for my unconscious mind and for the power of prayer. But what I object to in this approach is the passivity and fatalism that it entails. Prayer in the lives of the saints has always been a call to action, not a call to evade reality.

So the trouble with this approach is that it sees problems as things to be denied or evaded. The goal is the reality and nothing negative must be allowed to impinge on this reality. Now unfortunately if you deny the reality of problems, life is such that you are left with virtually nothing in real life that you are not denying.

The common factor in both the managerial and 'higher power' approaches to goal achievement (Push and Drift Modes by other names) is that both of them regard problems as enemies. One deals with problems by seeing them as enemies to be overcome, the other as enemies to be denied. The tactics are different but the basic orientation is the same.

So how about regarding problems as our friends to be welcomed?

Q Hmm . . . 'friends to be welcomed'. I don't often hear it put that way. Are you saying that problems are not really problems?

A *No, quite definitely not. What I mean is that we face up to the reality of a problem and see that very fact as an opportunity for growth and learning. In fact it is what we think of as problems, adversities and disappointments that provide the growth points in our lives and give us the impetus to progress. The stimulus of problems is what makes us alive. Life is about changing things that aren't the way we want them* *to be into things which are the way we want them to be. We share these characteristics with every living species, but as human beings we have much more sophisticated wants and much more sophisticated means of obtaining them.*

Q Very eloquent. But couldn't we progress even faster if we didn't have problems and setbacks?

A *Try and imagine if you can a world in which every desire you had was instantly gratified, in which there was no pain, no sorrow, nothing that wasn't exactly the way you wanted it. You would almost certainly find it inexpressibly boring. For every ten people who have read Dante's* Inferno *one has read his* Paradiso. *For every ten people who have read Milton's* Paradise Lost *one has read his* Paradise Regained.

Q I don't think I've ever heard of anyone who has read *Paradise Regained*.

A *Most people find the standard image of heaven – sitting around on a cloud with a harp – extremely unattractive.*

Q True.

A *The fact is that we need problems - what are games but artificially induced problems?*

Q OK, you win. I agree, we need problems! So what are the implications of this?

A *It means we can make an important shift in our thinking by beginning to think of the circumstances of our lives as friendly whatever they are.*

Q On the basis that the bigger the problem the bigger the learning?

A *Yes, though obviously that applies only within certain limits. There's not going to be much learning if the problem is totally overwhelming or even terminal.*

Q Well, my problem at the moment is that it's time to go to bed. So let's pursue this further tomorrow. And by the way, we've managed another 2,500 words today!

A *We have? Oh, yes, so we have. At this rate we'll finish the book in another two weeks!*

Saturday, 25 August – Attracting opportunities

Q So what's better today?

A *Well, on the well-ordered front I succeeded in doing the washing up whenever it was necessary.*

Q Good, and how did you get on with the telephone calls?

A *Yes, I still acted on phone calls immediately. That was good again.*

Q And getting important things done?

A *Yes, everything that really needed to be done got done.*

Q That's brilliant! So you already have got three areas well ordered, and this seems to be happening naturally?

A *Yes, I don't have to force myself to do them at all.*

Q What other areas are you well ordered in?

A *Well, obviously writing this book, and keeping the daily 'What's Better?' list – I really look forward to that. What else? Oh, yes, I cut a bit of the garden hedge every day – but I've never had a problem doing that.*

Q That's great – so you're making pretty good progress expanding the areas in which you are well ordered?

A *Yes, but I've still got a long way to go – you should see the state of my office!*

Q What do you think is the likelihood that you will soon have a perfectly ordered office?

A *Oh, I think it's pretty high. I've really been impressed by how once something goes on the 'What's Better?' list it seems to stick in my mind somehow.*

Q What are you doing that is making this happen?

A *Well, I am quite deliberately holding off forcing myself to get things sorted out. Whenever I get panicky and think I* ought *to be doing* *something about it, I just think to myself, 'I'll do it when I feel like doing it and not before.' And since I'm already seeing some powerful effects from working that way in other areas, I find it fairly easy to stop worrying about it.*

Q **Right! Tell me about these powerful effects in other areas.**

A *Yesterday I had a long conversation with the managing director of a company. He set the company up in conjunction with a well-known self-help author. He is keen to have me working with them on ways of forming a community of coaches that the company can draw on to work with their growing list of corporate clients.*

Q **That's great. What would you be doing in that?**

A *Well, I'd be organising the recruiting of coaches and we hope we'd make it into a byword for coaching excellence.*

Q **Am I right in thinking that this is very much in line with your vision for the future?**

A *On the face of it, yes. It seems to fit like a glove!*

Q **What are the ways in which it would fit?**

A *It means I could cut back my coaching clients to the numbers I want, have time for writing and thinking, and get really involved in organising something. And hopefully it would be highly profitable too!*

Q **Fantastic! And did this just fall out of the sky?**

A *Well it did originally, yes. He first approached me a few months ago. But the ideas have been very vague up to now. Suddenly it seems to have got much more concrete.*

Q **So you can really see this happening?**

A *It is a proposal that points directly towards my vision. And even if it didn't work out there doesn't seem to be much of a downside for me. And there's something else.*

Q **Yes?**

A *You know the course I have decided to go on in the States in October, but was concerned about the cost?*

Q **Yes.**

A *I told him how much of an advantage it would have for his company if I went, and he seemed quite willing to subsidise my going on it.*

Q **Is it my imagination or are things happening very fast all of a sudden?**

A *Yes, I can hardly believe the ways in which things are working out. In fact it's really beginning to get quite spooky. And by pure coincidence I am having coffee in Brighton this morning with the UK President of the International Coach Federation. This is something I can start making noises to him about.*

Q **Don't tell me . . . he just rang up and suggested you got together?**

A *Yes, a couple of days ago!*

Q **So what is it that you are doing that is attracting all these things? Obviously you are not planning them.**

A *That's right. I could never have planned for things to turn out the way they have. It's as if when things are ready to happen they just fall into place.*

Q **Just fall into place?**

A *Yes, I had terrible trouble when* Get Everything Done *was published because people kept contacting me to ask how one went about getting a book published. And all I could say was, 'I don't know – it just happened!'*

Q **So there wasn't much you could tell them about how they could go about it?**

A *No, in fact it was even worse than that because at the time the book was published I had some really positive major press coverage about my coaching. This was a huge boost to the book so people kept contacting me about how I managed my publicity as well.*

Q And how did you manage your publicity?

A *Well I didn't. It was complete coincidence that those articles came out at exactly the right time. They had nothing to do with the book at all.*

Q Nothing at all?

A *Nothing directly. But of course they were about the same subject – time management – and if you followed the thread of how they came about you could see that everything resulted from the actions I was taking to follow my vision.*

Q Was that the same vision you have now?

A *No, in those days I had three major goals. These were quite clear in my mind even though I hadn't actually written them down. I wanted to crack the time management problem that I had suffered from all my life, I wanted to become a great coach, and I wanted to write. In fact the strange thing is that initially the three goals were quite distinct. It wasn't till some way down the line that they became intertwined.*

Q What were you doing that made that happen?

A *I didn't plan anything. I just spent an awful lot of time experimenting with time management techniques and inventing new ones. And an awful lot of time getting as involved as I could in the life-coaching world – which in those days, a few years ago, was very new in this country. And an awful lot of time writing stuff – mainly for myself. And then I started giving time management seminars for fellow coaches, and as a result I got an invitation to write a book about time management and everything started coming together.*

Q So even though you didn't plan anything, you were still taking a lot of action?

A *Yes, and then I started analysing why everything had come together in the way it did and I started working out the principles on which this book is based. If you like, this book is my answer to those people who asked me, 'How do you get a book published?' or 'How do you handle your publicity?'*

Q Your answer to the question, 'How do you go about doing anything?' in fact.

A *That's right. These principles are applicable to anything that anyone sets out to do.*

Q Would now be a good time to do another summary?

A *Yes, good idea!*

Summary – Attaining your vision

- To get a powerful vision, use the four elements of:
  1. Feelings – our true motivators.
  2. Writing – write the vision down.
  3. Repetition – write it down regularly.
  4. Revision – keep revising it.
- To get the vision to pull you towards it, use:
  1. The vision itself.
  2. The Present Reality – write this using the same four elements.
- If your vision is pulling you towards it, you will find yourself acting effortlessly.
- Action in pursuance of a strong vision attracts opportunities.
- Problems and set-backs are friends because they:
  1. are the points at which real growth and learning take place;
  2. increase the tension between the Present Reality and the goal.
- This method of attaining a vision relies on the mind's powerful unconscious processing. However, the mind has two specialist tools it can avail itself of when appropriate:
  1. Planning;
  2. Rational linear thought.

Q Thanks for doing that. It's useful to see where we have got to. It's also raised a lot of questions in my mind which I would like to clarify with you.

A *Go ahead!*

Q **Well, first an observation. I like the idea that it's the mind's unconscious processing that should be regarded as the dominant way of thinking. And planning and conscious thought as specialist tools which are subservient to it. For most people, planning and conscious thought would be thought of as the ideal and unconscious thought as a cop-out.**

A *Yes, but whatever they* say *they believe, the reality is that they are actually acting from their unconscious processing. That's why people often know intellectually what action they should be taking but never succeed in doing it. And we all know how easy it is to rationalise a decision or an action when it's transparently obvious to everyone else why we've done it. The trouble is that when people deny the validity of unconscious thought they are depriving themselves of having any control over it. Once you accept your unconscious thought processes and put them at the service of a strong vision, you are beginning to have a force to be reckoned with.*

Q **OK, I follow that. Secondly, you talk about 'attracting' opportunities. What exactly do you mean by that? Is there some sort of extra-sensory perception or occult magnetism involved or what?**

A *To my way of thinking, it's more a case of the mind acting as a very powerful filter. Once it's targeted on a particular subject it will notice everything which is to do with that subject. I think there are millions of opportunities that float past us every day. And the mind has the capability to recognise and draw to our attention the ones that fit what we want.*

Q **Can you give an example?**

A *I've already mentioned how we notice cars of the same make and model when we buy a new car. Another example from my own experience is what happened when I became interested in bird-watching many years ago. There is one particular bird, the yellowhammer, which has a distinctive song called* 'A Little Bit of Bread and No Cheese'.

Anyway until I became interested in bird-watching I'd never consciously seen or heard a yellowhammer. But suddenly I began to see and hear them everywhere I went. The whole countryside became populated with yellowhammers. Then after a couple of years I lost interest in bird-watching and I've never seen or heard a yellowhammer since!

Q So you are saying that in the same way the mind picks up on opportunities when it has been properly targeted?

A *Yes, exactly that. The opportunities are always with us – it's just that we don't see them.*

Q Right. Now, from what I am understanding, this book is about how to make the most of the incredible power of unconscious thinking. And you are giving a basic method which anyone can follow?

A *Yes, that's right. By using the Goal Achievement Method, dialoguing, and the 'What's Better?' list.*

Q The thing that worries me is that these are all writing based. Now that's fine for you because you love writing – but that doesn't apply to everyone by a long shot!

A *That's an extremely good point. I suppose one answer would be that no methods are going to be suitable for everyone and that the people who are going to be attracted to this book are likely to be the ones who would benefit from it.*

Q Good cop-out answer!

A *Yes, isn't it! Perhaps a better answer would be that I believe that these methods are powerful enough for anyone to benefit from them very quickly and that one of the effects that using these methods will have is that people will then be empowered to design methods that will fit them more precisely.*

Q That's more like it. So for instance someone who was more at home talking than writing might find themselves doing the exercises into a tape-recorder?

A *I think something like that might easily come out of the dialoguing process.*

Q **Now I've got a really radical suggestion. Why don't we do a role play? You play someone who's read this book, loves the principles but finds the writing exercises really don't suit them, and I'll play her Future Self.**

A *A play within a play! Why not?*

Q **She'll need a vision and Present Reality.**

A *And a name!*

Q **This is going to be interesting.**

A *And I haven't got the faintest idea what is going to come out of it.*

Role play – Janet

The vision

I've developed my own ways of accessing my unconscious thinking and putting it at the service of my vision. I am moving forward so powerfully now that it's incredibly exciting.

Present Reality

I've read Mark's book and I love the way he describes what using the mind's unconscious powers has done for him and could do for me, but I really can't face the thought of having to do all that writing every day. Yet I feel that if I don't I am going to be missing out on something big.

Q **Hello, Janet. What can I do for you?**

A *This is all very strange to me. I am impressed by what the book says can happen if I use my unconscious mind, but I don't think there's any way*

I can do all that writing and exercises. I've got far too much on my plate anyway. And I hate writing. I'm just no good at it and it bores me to tears.

Q You seem to be doing a pretty good job at writing now.

A *Yes, I can do it for a bit. But it's a struggle. I wish there was some other way that I could access this without having to do all this.*

Q Do you recognise what Mark is talking about in the book? Does it ring any bells with you?

A *Yes, I do. I know what he means about doing things when you feel really enthusiastic and how easy it is. And how terribly difficult it is to do things when you are just forcing yourself the way he says. I hate doing that. But I've got so much on my plate what choice do I have?*

Q It sounds as if you do quite a few things which you are enthusiastic about.

A *Yes, I love doing things like going to the gym and taking time to be with myself. And going out for meals. But I just never get time to do them.*

Q What is happening when you do have time?

A *Sometimes I just say to myself, 'I'm going to do this no matter what.' I don't care whether I get the work done or not. And I usually feel glad that I did that, even though the work doesn't go away. But it's good to forget about it for a while.*

Q How do you go about forgetting about it?

A *It's like I make a decision to put it to one side. Like I stepped over a barrier or something and the work is the other side of the barrier.*

Q And what's it like on your side of the barrier?

A *It's a sense of freedom. Doesn't last for long though.*

Q What's the longest you remember it lasting?

A *When we went on holiday last without the children. We got away for a weekend.*

Q **That's great. So you managed to arrange a weekend away?**

A *Yes, it was really fun. My husband got away from his work too.*

Q **And are there times during the normal week when you get this sense of freedom?**

A *Yes, just times when I suddenly realise that I can choose what I can do for the next few minutes. I usually sit down and have a cup of tea, or phone a friend.*

Q **You do them because you feel like doing them?**

A *Yes, just because they're something I choose to do.*

Q **If you wanted to have more times like that how do you think you might go about it?**

A *I think I'd just learn to watch out for them more. Be more aware of when I could do something I want to do.*

Q **So that's a bit like what Mark talks about in the 'What's Better?' list?**

A *Hey, yes. I guess I don't have to write it down – just learn to watch out for them and sort of take a mental note.*

Q **OK, and the next time we talk you can tell me all about it.**

A *Well, that's fine but I don't think I'm going to be able to keep up all this writing.*

Q **Sure, can you just imagine a place in your mind that is your Future Self?**

A *I suppose I could do that, yes.*

Q **Then all you have to do is tell that place in your mind what's been better. Would you be able to do that?**

A *Yes, that's easy I guess.*

Q Well, that was fun. Where do you reckon she got to with that?

A *I think as long as she keeps looking for what's getting better, she'll begin to access the unconscious mind more and more.*

Q OK, let's leave it there for today. How many words did we write today?

A *Just over 3,000.*

Q Another for the list! Now tomorrow is Sunday and that's the day that you've set aside for the first update of your vision and Present Reality. So let's kick off with that tomorrow, shall we?

A *Yes, fine.*

Sunday, 26 August – Self-coaching

The vision

No change

Present Reality update

Since taking the decision to start my book again from scratch I have written 15,652 words in five days, an average of 3,130 words a day. I am delighted at what I have written so far.

I have seminars booked for September which will more than fill the gap in income left through letting the number of my clients run down.

I have some exciting proposals from a company which could take me a long way towards achieving my vision.

I have a strong possibility of getting my attendance at an expensive course subsidised.

I have succeeded in living five days without doing anything unless I feel like doing it. Although this has resulted in some backlogs building up I am gradually moving to allowing my vision of a well-ordered life pull me towards it. So far I have extended this to telephone calls, washing up and tidying the office.

Q That's a pretty impressive list of achievements for only five days. Tell me, what would you have thought if I had shown you that list last Wednesday when we started?

A *I would have thought it would have been quite impossible to achieve all that. I just can't believe it's all happened.*

Q Well, that's what happens when you have a good coach!

A *I absolutely agree. There's no doubt in my mind that this dialogue has had a profound effect on me.*

Q **In that case, perhaps this would be a good time to have a closer look at dialoguing. This is one of the cornerstones of your method, isn't it?**

A *Yes, the three essential parts of my method are the Goal Achievement Method, dialoguing and the 'What's Better?' list.*

Q **And do you recommend doing all three of them at the same time?**

A *Yes, very much so. All three work together to produce an effect which is greater than the sum of its parts.*

Q **That may be true but doesn't it take up more time than most people are going to be able to afford?**

A *How much time was that list of achievements at the beginning of today worth? How could I have used the time better?*

Q **Good point, but the fact is that many people won't even give it a try if it seems like too much of an effort.**

A *OK, I'll give you that. But let's just look at the time commitment involved. The vision and Present Reality only need to be looked at weekly, or less often once they have been established. And it only takes a maximum of ten minutes or so.*

Q **Right, that shouldn't put too many people off then.**

A *The daily 'What's Better?' list only takes a few minutes to write. In fact I add to mine during the day as I go along, so it really doesn't take any time at all.*

Q **OK, that just leaves the dialoguing. You are not seriously expecting everyone to write 2,500 words a day, are you?**

A *No of course not.* We *are using the dialogue to write the book with. So most of what we are writing is about principles. If you just look at the bits in which you are coaching me about my own real-time issues, you can see that they are really quite short.*

Q **So what sort of time commitment are we talking about here realistically. Half an hour a day?**

A *No, less than that. Probably fifteen to twenty minutes. It's best if the dialogue is written out as quickly as possible in a stream of consciousness way, without editing or worrying about grammar, punctuation, etc. We're going a bit slower than that because we* do *have to make it reasonably presentable.*

Q **What is happening that makes dialoguing so powerful for you?**

A *It seems to pull everything together that the other two methods are achieving. At the same time, without the other two methods I don't think it would have anything to focus on.*

Q **So it's as if the three methods are multiplied together rather than just added to each other?**

A *Yes, that's a good way to put it. And the other thing is that you are such a good coach. I'd like to spend a bit of time looking at the way you coach me.*

Q **OK, what do you notice particularly about my style?**

A *Well, the first thing I've noticed is that you never ever ask me what's wrong or what problems I have. You always focus on what I've been doing right and what's going well.*

Q **How does that work for you?**

A *Just brilliantly. I find that the focus on what I've been doing right inspires me no end. And even when I come up with a problem, you encourage me to find a bit that's going right.*

Q **Can you give an example of that?**

A *Yes, I mentioned that my biggest problem with trusting my feelings to tell me when to do things was that I didn't often feel like keeping my office well ordered. So you encouraged me to find one thing, however tiny, that I have done better each day about keeping things well ordered.*

Q What else have you noticed about my coaching style?

A *I've noticed you never give the answers. You always let me do that.*

Q How does that work?

A *Just like you're doing at the moment. You keep asking me questions about how I do things. When something is working for me you want to know what's happening, what's making it work, what I'm doing that's making it happen that way. I guess that helps me to realise that I'm in charge.*

Q What else do you notice?

A *You always ask me every day what's been better since we last talked. Somehow knowing that you are going to ask that really gets me going!*

Q Except that I haven't asked it today.

A *No more you have! Hey, I've had a great idea. Why don't you coach me now on my real-time issues and then we can go through it and highlight the techniques you are using?*

Q OK. But one question I'd like to ask you before we do that is how does my coaching style differ from your own?

A *Actually one of the things I've started doing since these dialogues began is imitating your style. And that's been having a noticeable effect on my clients. Not that I'm as good at it yet as you are!*

Q OK, what are you doing different now from what you used to?

A *I think the biggest problem I've always had as a coach is that I've been far too centred on what's wrong with the client's life and how to put it right. So the shift I am making is to find out what's right with the client's life and how to get more of it.*

Q And there you are again, telling me about your problems!

A *Touché! So what I am suggesting we do now is have a session on my real-life prob . . ., sorry, issues, and then we can go back over it again and put in some remarks in bold type. This is all so that people can see the best ways to coach themselves when doing these dialogues.*

Q **Let's get going then. What's been better since we talked yesterday?**

A *Well, on the being well-ordered front, the thing I put on my 'What's Better?' list yesterday was that I tidied my office.*

Q **Great, I noticed you put that on the Present Reality update. And how are you doing with the other things that you had on the list before?**

A *They are all still going great. I've washed up when I've felt like it, made phone calls when I've felt like it and cut the hedge when I've felt like it, and the result is they've all got done without any fuss.*

Q **That's fantastic! What do you think you might do to extend this even further?**

A *Well, the two big backlogs still remaining are e-mails and my in-tray. Then I need to get my systems for things like filing and invoices going. Somehow I find it difficult to imagine ever feeling like doing filing and invoices!*

Q **Well, if this resistance is your mind giving you a strong message about this, what would the message be?**

A *I suppose my mind is telling me it's about time I got someone else to do it! What's the point of struggling to do something myself that I don't enjoy and am no good at?*

Q **That's a great realisation! What could you do to get this moving?**

A *Now I come to think of it, I already asked my wife if I could pay her to do the invoices for me and she was very willing. It's just that I never got round to organising it!*

Q **Great! Are there other ways she might be willing to help you with this?**

A *Yes, I'm sure she would, and it would be nice to be able to involve her more with what I am doing.*

Q If we were to ask her about this, what do you think she would say?

A *I'm sure she'd be delighted. She likes to feel part of what I'm up to.*

Q That's great! I'm looking forward to hearing how you take this forward . . . And now let's replay this dialogue and I'll put my comments on what I'm doing in bold type.

Q Let's get going then. **(Finding out what's working:)** What's been better since we talked yesterday?

A *Well, on the being well-ordered front, the thing I put on my 'What's Better?' list yesterday was that I tidied my office.*

Q **(Affirming:)** Great, I noticed you put that on the Present Reality update. **(Finding out what's working:)** And how are you doing with the other things that you had on the list before?

A *They are all still going great. I've washed up when I've felt like it, made phone calls when I've felt like it and cut the hedge when I've felt like it, and the result is they've all got done without any fuss.*

Q **(Affirming:)** That's fantastic! **(Extending what's working:)** What do you think you might do to extend this even further?

A *Well the two big backlogs still remaining are e-mails and my in-tray. Then I need to get my systems for things like filing and invoices going. Somehow I find it difficult to imagine ever feeling like doing filing and invoices!*

Q **(Finding out what the mind is saying:)** Well, if this resistance is your mind giving you a strong message about this, what would the message be?

A *I suppose my mind is telling me it's about time I got someone else to do it! What's the point of struggling to do something myself that I don't enjoy and am no good at?*

Q **(Affirming:)** That's a great realisation! **(Extending what the mind is saying:)** What could you do to get this moving?

A *Now I come to think of it, I already asked my wife if I could pay her to do the invoices for me and she was very willing. It's just that I never got round to organising it!*

Q **(Affirming:)** Great! **(Finding out what works:)** Are there other ways she might be willing to help you with this?

A *Yes, I'm sure she would, and it would be nice to be able to involve her more with what I am doing.*

Q **(Looking at situation from another person's point of view:)** If we were to ask her about this, what do you think she would say?

A *I'm sure she'd be delighted. She likes to feel part of what I'm up to.*

Q **(Affirming:)** That's great! **(Handing back control:)** I'm looking forward to hearing how you take this forward.

Q What would you say most characterised my approach?

A *Well, I think what you are doing is totally respecting the way the mind works. You are helping my mind to identify what is working and to seek out ways of making it work even better. So it is a method of helping to access the unconscious processing powers of the mind.*

Q And how does it fit in with your 'pull' theory?

A *Absolutely great, because it is a way of speeding up the process by helping the mind to integrate what is happening even faster. By having two aspects of my mind engage in this sort of questioning it seems to enable the mind to be able to make connections more quickly. What I think is happening is that it is integrating the functions of the conscious and unconscious minds so that they are working together rather than in opposite directions.*

Q And would it work as well if it were a real person asking the questions?

A *Yes, I think so. As I said I have actually started to imitate your techniques in my own work with clients. And I think it has improved my coaching. I think the advantage of having a real coach as opposed to coaching yourself is that the coach may be able to see things that the client is completely blind to or is trying to hide from themselves. On the other hand self-coaching can be much more frequent and more immediate. So they complement each other. I certainly don't intend to cease working with my real-life coach just because I am doing self-coaching as well.*

Q Do you see other ways in which this dialoguing technique could be used?

A *Yes, I think one can use one's imagination here. We have already used a role play to gain insights into how another person might react to a certain situation.*

Q Yes, and you mentioned earlier something you want to do towards the end of the book, which is to expand your own vision of the future by role playing your Future Self being coached by his Future Self.

A *Yes, I'm looking forward to that one.*

Q Are there ways in which this might be used to gain insights into your relationships with other people?

A *That's an interesting thought. Perhaps we could explore that tomorrow. In the meantime what I would really like to do now is to summarise what we have discussed again, particularly the techniques for self-coaching.*

Self-coaching techniques

- The aim of self-coaching is to integrate the conscious and unconscious functions of the mind by:

1. identifying what is working,
2. then expanding it.

- Self-coaching works in close collaboration with the 'What's Better?' list.
- Techniques that can be used include:
  1. Asking questions to identify:
     a. What is working or has worked in the past,
     b. What is happening when it works,
     c. How it can be extended further.
  2. Affirming what has worked.
  3. Identifying messages from the mind, e.g. resistance giving a red light.
  4. Giving control back to the mind to take things forward.
- Typical questions include:
  1. What's been better since we last spoke?
  2. What has been working?
  3. Have there been times that have been better than others?
  4. What are you doing when things are working better?
  5. What could you do to make that happen more often?
  6. If your resistance to doing this were a strong message from your mind, what would that message be?
- For a specific issue, give an assignment of identifying something each day about that issue to go on the 'What's Better?' list.

Q OK, that's great. And we've done another 2,600 words today.

A *That's fantastic. I'm really looking forward to seeing what happens next week. Do you think we'll have as many impressive gains to put on the Present Reality update next Sunday as we had today?*

Q I have no idea. But it's important not to get too hung up on racking up huge gains all the time. Remember what we were saying about problems and set-backs being the times of greatest growth.

A *Thanks for reminding me about that. Anyway, tomorrow is a bank holiday and I have no appointments all day so it'll be an excellent opportunity to forge ahead with the writing.*

Monday, 27 August – Long-term vision

Q What's been better since we last spoke?

A *On the self-organisation front, I really have hardly anything to report. I had to scratch around to think of* anything *I had done better yesterday. In the end the only item I could think of was that I had kept my office tidy for two days running.*

Q That sounds pretty good to me. You are consolidating the gains you have made. How did you succeed in doing that?

A *I'm resolved to only do things when I feel like doing them, and late last night I just felt I couldn't possibly go to bed with my desk untidy. So I put everything away. I didn't take long and it gave me a great sense of satisfaction.*

Q That's great. How well did you maintain the other things to do with self-organisation?

A *Well, it was a Sunday and there weren't any phone calls. The washing up got done without any reluctance. It was good it just got done when it needed to be done.*

Q That's what you've always wanted, isn't it? To want to do things at the same time as they need to be done? Congratulations, it sounds as if you are getting there!

A *Yes, I'm perfectly organised at washing dishes . . . perhaps I'm in the wrong job! But seriously I have a huge backlog of e-mails building up. It starts from the time we started this dialogue; so it's about six days long now. I've dealt with the urgent replies but there's still lots of stuff in there that needs actioning. And the same applies to paperwork, though there's not quite so much of it.*

Q You don't sound too worried about it.

A *No, it was a deliberate decision to let it build up if necessary. I have always kept pretty well up to date with e-mail, but only by using various time management techniques. This time I was determined to* *do e-mail only when I felt like doing it. I'm glad I made that decision, but I haven't felt like clearing my e-mail yet. And of course, the longer I don't feel like it, the bigger the backlog gets and the less I feel like doing it.*

Q Well, congratulations on sticking to your decision. What do you see happening here?

A *I think there will come a point when I can't stand to see it building up any more and then I will start hacking away at it. So it will have to get worse before it gets better.*

Q And once you do start 'hacking away at it', what do you think the chances are that you will be able to keep it organised.

A *I have a feeling that it may not be too difficult. Once I've put some action on the 'What's Better?' list, I think it will probably be like writing the book. What I was resisting before suddenly becomes something that I can do without any resistance at all.*

Q So you are pretty hopeful?

A *Yes, and you know what . . . ?*

Q No.

A *This conversation seems to be having the effect of making me want to start on my e-mail!*

Q Okaaay! Let's pause a bit then!

(later)

Q So how did that go?

A *Fine. I cleared out all the e-mails that would take less than two minutes to action. It took me about an hour to do that, which wasn't too bad. Now I've got a much smaller number to take action on and I know what they are and what needs doing. So I'm not completely up to date with my e-mail yet. But I do have a significant advance to record on the 'What's Better?' list.*

Q Well done! You're extending the territory and consolidating the gains. That's really good. But I'd like us to move on from getting well-organised. What else has been better in your life as a whole?

A *Something happened yesterday, and I'm not sure whether it's a terrible failure or whether it's a success.*

Q Sounds intriguing! What happened?

A *Well, yesterday was a Sunday and today is a bank holiday. So I'd basically got two days with nothing in my diary at all. I had great plans for all the work I was going to succeed in doing as a result.*

Q Yes, nothing like a holiday for catching up with work!

A *Exactly! That's why I'm not sure whether this is a success or a failure. What happened is that I went into my son's room (he's left home now but he still has his old room here) and saw a thriller on his bookshelf. It was one of those very thick paperbacks – the sort of book that people read on long airplane journeys. Anyway I picked it up and started looking at it, and found I couldn't put it down. The long and the short of it is that I read the* entire *book from cover to cover and it took me just about the whole day, and I did absolutely nothing else all day.*

Q Except write 2,600 words and do the washing up?

A *You're laughing at me! Yes, those things seem to be so well-established now that I would have quite a struggle* not *to do them.*

Q That's interesting. So you are now getting to the stage where some of the things you were resisting before are now becoming what you *want* to do on a regular ordered basis?

A *Yes, once I'd listened to what my resistance was saying about writing my book, it was like taking a cork out of a bottle.*

Q Right. And so let's try listening to what happened in this thriller episode. If setbacks are times of learning and growth, what message has this for you?

A *Well, I think it was partly my mind telling me that it didn't want to work on a Sunday. And perhaps I need to listen to myself more about taking proper time off.*

Q Good point. What else?

A *I think it was something of a test too. It was as if my mind were saying, 'Let's see how really committed you are to doing what you feel like doing. Here's a completely useless activity. Do it for as long as you feel like doing it. Don't force yourself to do anything more constructive.'*

Q That's interesting.

A *Yes, because several times I remember saying to myself, 'I really ought to be doing something else,' and then I'd say, 'But this is what I feel like doing and I'm going to go on doing it for as long as I feel like it.'*

Q That word *ought* again.

A *Yes, indeed! So in a way I feel it wasn't a defeat at all, but something of a triumph. Like I was actually prepared to do an entirely useless activity all day and not feel guilty about it.*

Q So it's a bit like taking exercise. Would it be possible to invent a more useless activity than cycling on a stationary bicycle? But the whole point is the effect that the activity has on you.

A *Yes, that's right.*

Q What else might this episode be telling you?

A *To keep the exercise metaphor going, I think it taught me that I prefer real-life cycling to riding a stationary bicycle. There are loads of things I prefer doing to reading trashy thrillers. In fact the really sad thing about this episode is that I didn't particularly enjoy it.*

Q So it might be a first step to freeing yourself to do more of what you really do enjoy?

A *Yes, and that really would be a triumph!*

Q Any other messages for you from this episode?

A *Hmmm . . . I did have a really odd thought there. If setbacks are growth and learning opportunities, then perhaps they should get recorded on the 'What's Better?' list.*

Q How could you make that a constructive thing to do?

A *I get it! I should record the growth and learning that comes from the setback. That is, find the positive things that are coming out of what appears to be a negative experience.*

Q Didn't I tell you that there is always *something* better?

A *Yes, that's beginning to make more sense now.*

Q So how could you positively record this on your 'What's Better?' list?

A *Let's see:*

- *I allowed myself to do an entirely pointless activity all day without feeling guilty.*
- *I did not allow myself to be pressured into doing what I ought to be doing.*
- *I took an important step towards freeing myself to do what I really enjoy.*
- *I listened to my mind about allowing myself adequate time off.*

Q Great! Let's move on. What else is better?

A *Yes, one little interesting thing happened when I went to bed last night. I always set my alarm clock, even on days off. And last night I just seemed to have a little voice in my head saying, 'Don't set the alarm clock. Just get up when you feel like it.'*

Q And when did you feel like it?

A *The interesting thing is that I got up about the time I would have* *anyway. But there was a quite different feel to it. Instead of feeling that I* had *to get up, I felt that I was getting up because I* wanted *to get up.*

Q That's great!

A *Yes, I seem to be learning to release myself from having to control everything. I don't think I realised how much I do that. The real challenge of course will be to not set my alarm clock on a work day.*

Q Do you feel that you *ought* not to set your alarm clock?

A *Aaagh! You got me! Of course I should set my alarm clock if I feel like setting my alarm clock, and not set it if I don't feel like setting it!*

Q You really are beginning to learn.

A *I do have a question about all this though. I hope you can help me think it through.*

Q OK, what is it?

A *Well, it's fine for me as a self-employed person to sit around waiting until I feel like doing my e-mails, but what about people who are in employment and have to get on with things whether they like it or not?*

Q That's a very good question. Let's have a look at it. You've recently made the change from being employed to being self-employed, so you have recent experience of both worlds. What's the most significant difference between the two?

A *That's easy. As a self-employed person I am working for myself and whether I'm successful or not it's my show and no one else's.*

Q And how does that affect the work you do?

A *I probably work harder than ever. But I don't mind because it's* my *work.*

Q So being self-employed doesn't mean that you do less work than an employed person?

A *No, far from it, because I don't have all the back-up that an employed person has. I have to do everything myself or at the very least arrange* *for everything to be done. There's no marketing department, or human resources department, or finance department, etc. etc. It's all me.*

Q So you can't afford to sit around waiting until you feel like doing your e-mails either?

A *Even less, probably. Because these things directly affect my pocket, while an employed person has the cushion of a salary. They really have to mess things up in order to get fired, and even then there's all sorts of employment protection legislation, etc. I don't have anything like that. If I mess it up with a client, I've lost a good chunk out of my pay, period.*

Q So if this is all true how come you are willing to go through this process of waiting until you are ready?

A *Because I can see how totally vital it is. If I end up* wanting *to do things when they need to be done, I will have made a gigantic step forward in productivity which will greatly outweigh the disadvantage of getting a few days behind with my e-mails. And what sort of employees would you prefer to have? Ones who only do what you tell them and only then because they are frightened of getting the sack, or ones who have a powerful vision and are doing their work for you because they* want *to do it?*

Q Yes, very true. And come to that which sort of employee would you prefer to be?

A *I think the big distinction here is between Pull Mode and Drift Mode. We are not talking about people sitting around aimlessly. We are talking about people who are going somewhere, but know that doesn't necessarily mean rushing around being busy the whole time.*

Q I think you've succeeded in answering your question!

A *Yes, I think I have.*

Q We mentioned yesterday that we might look at how dialoguing might be used in connection with one's relationships with other people, but there's something I'd like to look at first. I want to

go back to the question of how one sets a powerful vision in the first place.

A *Yes?*

Q You've described how to set goals and progress towards them using the Goal Achievement Method. But the examples you gave were quite short-term ones.

A *Yes, I said it was a good idea to start with something short-term in order to practise the method.*

Q But your own vision is quite long-term. At least I assume it's intended to be long-term, though it doesn't have any date attached to it. What sort of timescale did you intend when you wrote it?

A *I was thinking in terms of three to five years, though things are beginning to happen so fast now that it might be shorter. I think I'm reluctant to put a timescale on it because that in itself is limiting. I did write some materials for my clients on this subject and perhaps now is a good time to bring them up.*

Q Yes, it would be useful to see them.

A *One thing I've noticed is that most of the problems people have with the Goal Achievement Method are to do with setting the right timescale for what they want to do.*

The future

Although we have looked at how to achieve short-term goals in the future, I have left dealing with long-term future goals until you have been able to get some short-term successes. Now that you have worked through the exercises I gave earlier you should be ready to look at a wider vista. You have of course already done some work on it earlier, when we had some exercises on finding out what you really want.

Now it's time to revisit this. We want to set some goals for our long-term future. The best timescale for this sort of goal is usually three to five years. This is long enough to achieve most goals, even the most ambitious.

Using the same method of goal writing that we have used in the other modules, you can now write out a description of what you want your life to be like in three to five years' time. Don't put a specific date on it but bear that sort of timescale in mind as you write the description. Incorporate every part of your life that is important to you.

Example

I am working in my office in my castle which has a magnificent panoramic view over a bay with yellow sand and a blue sea. It is a warm sunny climate and the light has a wonderful luminous quality about it. My office is a large airy room with a stone floor and walls with tapestries hanging on them.

There is a sense of spaciousness, calm and purposefulness – it feels like the hub of the universe. It is a beautiful place. I have twenty clients who are paying me a total of $1 million a year, with a waiting list of the rich and famous who want me as their adviser. A little further down the hill is my highly profitable training institute, where people are being trained to take my methods into the world. It is run for me by a team of enthusiastic trainers. I live a completely integrated life and achieve everything I set out to do with the greatest economy and creative power. I have great fun doing this and love my work and my life as a whole. I am changing the lives of thousands and am a major influence in the world. I am in total health and look and feel younger than I did ten years previously – and am much fitter than I was then.

If you have trouble deciding what you really want, just make it up. Imagine that you are a character in a novel and you are writing a happy ending for yourself (there will of course be sequels!).

Make sure while you are writing the goal that you don't worry about how to achieve the goal. The path to the goal will only come clear bit by bit after you have committed yourself to the goal. To check whether you have really arrived at what you want, ask yourself the question, 'Am I settling for second best here?' If you are then change it to the best you can imagine. After all, even if you didn't completely achieve your goal, you would have a much more interesting time pursuing the best with conviction than resigning yourself to never reaching beyond second best.

Quiz:
Who is going to get further?
a) The person who is half-heartedly pursuing a second-best goal, or
b) The person who is enthusiastically pursuing what they really want?

If you don't know the precise details of what you want then fill in as much as you can be sure of. For instance you may not know what type of work you want to do, but you might know how much you want to earn, whether you want to work for someone else, which of your skills or interests you would like to be using, and so on.

Once you have written this goal to your satisfaction, keep editing it at regular intervals. Make a game of adding new details and living with them for a bit. If you don't like them, you can always take them out again. Remember that the more you interact with this goal, the more it is going to impress itself on your mind.

Exercise 6.1
Write a goal for your future in three to five years in the way discussed above. Add your Present Reality and rewrite both regularly – daily to start off with and then at lengthening intervals as you feel your mind latch on to the goal.

Exercise 6.2

If you still have difficulty identifying what you really want then try this exercise. Imagine again that you are a character in your own novel and write out *three* alternative happy endings. Try to make each one as different as possible from the others. Just make sure that in each one your character ends up happy!

Once you have done this, compare them and try to identify what the common themes running through them are. Sometimes it helps to get a trusted friend or colleague to read them too. Often someone else can spot something that is glaringly obvious – except to you!

Once you have identified the common themes have a go at writing a goal that expresses these themes directly. You might for example find that in all your scenarios the common themes are expressing your creativeness, working for yourself, travel and finding a life partner. So write a goal something like this:

I am having a wonderful time travelling the world in connection with my own business. Through this I am able to express my creative skills to the full. My life partner shares this with me and together we have found a contentment that forms the background to everything we do.

You may think this is a very vague goal, but in fact it expresses clearly the major things that are important to you in life. When you have clarity about these you can then start to fill in some more of the details, but allow this process to happen naturally, don't try to force it.

Now all you have to do is sit back and let the goal manifest itself. Right?

Well, yes that is just about right – only don't imagine that it is an easy process. The most difficult part is keeping your faith in your goal. There will be times when everything seems to be going wrong, when you become discouraged, when you can see no way in which you can possibly reach the goal.

These are the crucial times. How you deal with them (and remember they *will* happen) makes the difference between reaching your goal and not reaching it. The biggest temptation you will face is to think that, because you can't see *how* to reach your goal, you don't really want the goal. But if you stick to the goal you will come through.

Remember:

- You *will* get discouraged at times.
- You *will* come to a grinding halt at times.
- Everything *will* seem to be against you at times.
- You *will* have to go backwards at times.

When these things happen, if you keep your goal alive, these periods will become the times you make the most growth towards your goal. Setbacks are in fact an essential part of the growth process. They are the times when you learn the most and will grow the most. And once you start to come out of the setback you will have renewed impetus.

But if you give up, you give up.

The most important thing to do in these periods of discouragement is to keep writing out your goal and to keep writing out the Present Reality. Be totally honest about your feelings when you are writing the Present Reality. As well as helping you to work through these feelings at the time, it will also provide an invaluable record for the future of how your mind works. If you start to become discouraged again in the future, you can look back and see that you've felt like this before *and* managed to come through.

Short-term goals

I have already said that the best timescale to concentrate on is three to five years. This is sufficient time to allow even the biggest life changes to take place, or at the least to be well established as directions in which you are going. The advantage of this timescale is that it gives direction to everything you do. By writing a narrative vision of where you want to be, you have ensured that your vision is integrated. It is important to include all the strands of your life in your vision.

With a clear overall vision there is often little need to set short-term goals. The problem with short-term goals is that they are often too prescriptive of how you are going to get to your vision. As soon as you start setting time targets and working out actions that need to be done by them you are committing yourself to a specific way of getting to where you want to be. You have ceased to allow your mind to be creative about achieving the goal.

Now of course I am well aware that many areas of human endeavour need detailed planning. You don't build a spaceship to take men to the moon without some extremely detailed and comprehensive plans and monitoring of the activities of thousands of people. Yet the space programme itself is a fine example of how important it is to get the vision right, and then the plans will follow. The key moment in the space mission was President Kennedy's speech in which he said 'We choose to go to the moon – we choose to go to the moon – we choose to go to the moon in this decade . . .' Without that strong visionary statement at the start, would the moon landings ever have taken place?

The vision itself will integrate your actions. Use plans when you need plans – which is usually when you have important deadlines or the actions of other people to coordinate. And similarly use sub-goals when you need them. As an example, if you have a vision one part of which consists of a perfect and well-ordered working environment, you might make a sub-goal of this if it shows little sign of progress after you have been working on the vision for some time.

Sub-goals are a tool that should be used sparingly. The reason for this is that the more goals you have at any one time the more your attention will be dispersed. It is easier for the brain to deal with a complete narrative picture which includes many different strands than for it to deal with several unrelated goals.

Let's go back to the vision that I gave as an example earlier in this module:

> I am working in my office in my castle which has a magnificent panoramic view over a bay with yellow sand and a blue sea. It is a warm sunny climate and the light has a wonderful luminous quality about it. My office is a large airy room with a stone floor and walls with tapestries hanging on them.
>
> There is a sense of spaciousness, calm and purposefulness – it feels like the hub of the universe. It is a beautiful place. I have twenty clients who are paying me a total of $1 million a year, with a waiting list of the rich and famous who want me as their adviser. A little further down the hill is my highly profitable training institute, where people are being trained to take my methods into the world. It is run for me by a team of enthusiastic trainers. I live a completely integrated life and achieve everything I set out to do with the greatest economy and creative power. I have great fun doing this and love my work and my life as a whole. I am changing the lives of thousands and am a major influence in the world. I am in total health and look and feel younger than I did ten years previously – and am much fitter than I was then.

If we break this down into its constituent parts, the sub-goals might look something like this:

1. To set up a training institute for self-development courses.
2. To recruit and train associates for duplicating the business.
3. To purchase a suitable property in a historic building.
4. To increase the profitability of my clients by 300%.
5. To improve working systems so that personal efficiency is increased by 60%.

6. To design and implement a health and physical fitness regime for myself with the intention of increasing effectiveness and lifespan.

Our minds find it far easier to relate to the narrative goal, which contains a strong integrated image, than to the discrete, unintegrated goals in the list. When the picture is one, the mind can start working to produce the entire picture. With itemised goals, each one is perceived as separate. The result is that they all become to some extent in competition with each other.

So whenever we start to set up sub-goals we are in part destroying the integrity of the whole picture. It's certainly advisable at times to set sub-goals, but don't use them to be the main motivators of your life. Always see them as putting a closer focus on a particular aspect of the main picture.

Example

While continuing to work on my three to five year vision (see page 81) I decide that I should concentrate specifically on getting my work life better organised. So I write a sub-goal which links in with the main vision. I decide to focus on the 'sense of spaciousness, calm and purposefulness' which the vision speaks of. So my sub-goal might go like this:

The vision

I am well ordered in everything I do, everything gets actioned immediately at just the right time and I am up to date with everything. This gives me a wonderful sense of spaciousness, calm and purposefulness.

Present Reality

At the moment I am surrounded by piles of paper, books on the floor, washing up in the sink, e-mail piling up, invoices not sent out, loads of things outstanding and a general sense

> of untidiness and of being behind. This drains me and diffuses my energies.

By the following day I was writing (for this is a genuine example):

> I made a huge advance yesterday in this. It was as if I had been seized with enthusiasm to get it done. I got my desk tidy, cleared all my e-mail and made huge inroads into my paper. I also got some administrative stuff sorted. Still lots to do, particularly as regards paper and tidiness, but a huge advance. And the great thing is I really wanted to do it.

The best rule to use is that, whatever level of goal you are working on, you should only be concentrating on one goal at a time. Make sure that one goal is imprinted on your mind before moving your focus closer in or further out.

Q That's very useful. I notice by the way that the vision wasn't quite the same as the one you are using now.

A *Yes, that's because I have revised it since writing that piece. Remember it is vital to keep engaging with the goal and revising it to fit better with what you really want.*

Q What is the main difference between that goal and the one you have now?

A *Two things. First I added more feelings to it. Second I realised I really didn't want to be coaching twenty clients. That wouldn't leave time for all the other things I want to be doing. So I thought four really good ones would be much better!*

Q Yes, I'm sure they would be! And the other thing I wanted to ask is how about deadlines? Is it useful to set yourself deadlines?

A *Most books about goal setting advise the use of deadlines in order to speed up the process. But personally I regard this with a certain amount* *of scepticism. There are of course deadlines which* have *to be met. But when it's a case of setting arbitrary target dates simply in order to put more pressure on ourselves, then I suspect it can be counter-productive.*

Q Why is that?

A *For a start, our minds are not easily fooled. If we know that the deadline is not really necessary then we are not going to persuade our minds to take it seriously. This means that when we fail to meet the deadline, we chalk it up as a failure even though things might have been progressing quite well up to that point.*

Q Do you have any experience of this happening?

A *Yes, I've given the Goal Achievement Method to hundreds of people and asked them to pick a project that would take a month or less. And what I found was that the relatively few people who said they had failed at their target had almost all actually made considerable advances – it was just that they hadn't met the one-month deadline. Without that deadline they would probably have been quite happy with their progress.*

Q So it encouraged them to look at what had gone wrong, rather than what had gone right?

A *Yes. That's right. And I have a second objection to deadlines, which is that our minds need time. Processing in the deeper unconscious levels of the mind is much slower than conscious thought (hence the book title* Hare Brain, Tortoise Mind*). Creation is not an instant process. Even God is depicted as taking six days to create the world. Setting deadlines may simply serve to produce unripe fruit. I think we are well advised to allow things to take the time that they need to come to fruition.*

Q Which may sometimes be *less* time than we think.

A *Yes, sometimes. So my advice is include a deadline in your goal when it really* has *to be achieved by a certain date, but otherwise leave the time period unspecified.*

Q **And talking about deadlines being limiting, we have just knocked up a total of 23,500 words, which is almost exactly where you had got to in the previous draft that you scrapped.**

A *So we've written as much in six days as it took me six months to write before!*

Q **A thirty-fold increase in productivity simply by getting the time right and listening to what your mind was saying instead of resisting it. Incredible!**

A *Since we've got plenty of time today, I'd really like to do a little more coaching on my real-time issues.*

Q **OK, what can I do for you?**

A *One of the big areas in my vision is the subject of health and fitness. It's crucial because there's not much point in achieving the rest of my vision if I'm not going to be healthy or if I'm going to be too tired to enjoy it.*

Q **You've made some huge advances here recently, haven't you?**

A *Yes, I lost twenty-eight pounds this year, and I've been walking regularly as exercise. But I just feel it's all a bit of a struggle. I'm not sure I want to be condemned to a lifetime of dieting and having to spend hours exercising every day.*

Q **How did you manage to lose all that weight?**

A *I just knew I was going to. It was like when I stopped smoking years and years ago. I'd given up smoking hundreds of times before, but that time I just knew I was never going to smoke again. And twenty-seven years later I never have.*

Q **So in the same way you knew the time was right for losing weight?**

A *Yes, I knew without a doubt that I'd lose the weight. The trouble is that I don't know without a doubt that I won't put it on again!*

Q What was different about losing the weight?

A *I just knew it. I don't think anything in the world would have stopped me from losing it. I seemed to be able to stick to the diet with the greatest of ease. But now I've got to the target I seem to have lost that drive.*

Q It's been a while since you hit the target, and you are still within acceptable limits of it. How have you managed to do that?

A *I've weighed myself every day, and lately I always write down in my 'What's Better?' list whenever I return within the limit I've set myself.*

Q That's great. So you're taking some pretty definite action to keep yourself there.

A *Yes, but I feel it's sort of very fragile somehow. That one day I would just find my weight had taken off again. It's happened before when I've lost weight. I just lose control of it all of a sudden.*

Q Lose control?

A *Yes, that was an interesting choice of words, wasn't it? Especially in the light of what I was saying earlier today about finding out how much I needed to control things. I suppose I could simply accept that my body knows what the best weight is for it and trust it to keep to it.*

Q What would you put in your 'What's Better?' list then?

A *I'd record the times I'd trusted my body to look after my weight, rather than the times I'd succeeded in controlling my weight!*

Q What's different about that?

A *The feeling of resistance has fallen away. It just feels completely different somehow.*

Q That's fantastic! It sounds to me that you've made a real advance there. Do you want to deal with the subject of exercise now or leave it till another time?

A *No, I'll leave it till later because right now I feel like going for a walk!*

(later)

Q How did you get on with the walk?

A *Very well. But I also finished dealing with all my e-mail.*

Q That's amazing! How did that happen?

A *Well, I just felt that I wanted to finish it off having got so far earlier.*

Q And how likely do you think it is that you will keep your e-mail up to date from now on?

A *Somehow it just doesn't seem to be an issue any more. I'm virtually certain that it'll just get cleared without fuss from now on.*

Q And how about exercise?

A *Again it's like my weight. I think I can just trust my body to know what exercise I need from now on.*

Q It sounds as if things are really coming together now.

A *I think so, yes.*

Q Don't forget to keep putting at least one thing that's better about being well ordered on your list each day. And of course you will be continuing to write down all the other things that are better about your life as well.

Tuesday, 28 August – Other people

A *Could you possibly coach me on a specific subject? I've got a coaching client coming up in an hour, and I feel I need some help.*

Q Certainly. How can I help you?

A *The problem is that all the dialoguing we have done and the advances I have made by being coached by you seem to have left me in a sort of half-way house as far as my own coaching is concerned.*

Q Can you tell me more about what you mean?

A *I'd developed a coaching style which I was comfortable with, but it's very different from the way you coach. My problem is that I want to coach like you but I'm worried about switching from what I'm used to into something that I'm not used to.*

Q I think you said that there were times when you'd found yourself imitating my style anyway? What were you doing differently when that happened?

A *I was doing things like asking them what was better since the last session and digging to find what they were doing well.*

Q And how did that work for you?

A *It seemed to get a good response. In fact I was delighted that some of my clients seemed to have made a lot more progress than normal.*

Q That's wonderful. What was happening there?

A *I expect they always made progress, but were more used to looking at their problems. Anyway, they really seemed proud of what they had done and determined to continue with their progress.*

Q That must have been a great feeling. And did this all happen quite naturally?

A *Yes, I found myself doing this almost without thinking about it. Like I said, I found myself imitating you.*

Q And this client you've got coming up, how can you extend that to what's been happening to him?

A *I suppose just let it happen naturally. Not try to force it.*

Q Good, I expect that will work very well. After the session, I recommend that you go back through it carefully and add as many things as possible to your 'What's Better?' list.

A *Thank you for that.*

Q No problem. Now tell me what's been better since we last spoke?

A *It's only a trivial thing, but I didn't set my alarm clock again last night. And today is a work day.*

Q And what happened?

A *I got up in plenty of time. But the interesting thing is that I didn't feel the need to get up hours early and do tons of work before breakfast. I've been doing that a lot lately. And that's one of the things that's made me feel I'm on a sort of treadmill, having to run just to stand still.*

Q So you're feeling far less pressurised? That's good.

A *Yes, somehow it's as if all the work has disappeared somewhere. I don't quite understand it.*

Q What's been happening that makes you feel that?

A *I think it's because I'm no longer worried about what I* ought *to be doing. I am beginning to have much more faith that if something needs to be done it will get done, but I don't have to worry about when I do it. And if I don't ever do it, then it didn't need to be done anyway.*

Q That's a great shift to have made. How could you extend that into more areas of your life?

A *I think the whole area of relating to other people is one. We've been meaning to talk about that.*

Q Yes, we have. I hadn't forgotten. How could you apply this shift to relating to other people?

A *I suppose there are two things. Stop telling myself I* ought *to be doing such and such because they expect it. And the converse of that is to stop putting expectations on other people.*

Q Telling them what *they* ought to be doing in other words?

A *Yes, though I may only be telling them in my own mind – I may never actually tell them face to face what they ought to be doing. But I guess they pick up subconsciously that that's what I'm thinking.*

Q And what sort of people does this apply to?

A *Oh, everyone. My wife, my children, my friends, clients, everyone.*

Q Have you had experience of this working in the past – not putting expectations on people, I mean?

A *Yes, when I've been willing to let people be themselves it's always improved our relationship enormously.*

Q What's happening there that makes it so much better?

A *I think it's like what happens when I free myself from the* oughts *in my life. It gives me freedom to grow. I think* oughts *actually imprison one in a particular state. So, in the same way, by freeing other people from expectations, I am freeing them to grow as well and that means freeing the relationship to grow too. Or sometimes move on.*

Q Who was it who said, 'Whenever someone gives you advice, remember that they have a secret motive – which is to make you more like them'?

A *I think it was me actually! But it's good you've reminded me of that because I think so often what we are trying to do with other people is imprison them within our own limitations.*

Q Now this raises an interesting question. How far can we include other people in our own vision?

A *Specific named people you mean?*

Q **Yes.**

A *I think what I'd like to do is write a short piece on this.*

Q **OK.**

How other people relate to our vision

Unless we are planning to become hermits, our vision for the future will always include other people. They will be filling various roles. For instance, in my opening vision there is an impressive cast of characters:

- Four clients, who are paying $1 million each.
- My team of trainers.
- The people being trained in my methods.
- Thousands of people around the world whose lives are being changed.

I have no specifically named candidates for any of these characters as yet. But if I am moving towards this vision and keep it alive, my mind will be attracting the right people to make it happen. And not only do I need the above cast of characters, but there will also be a shifting population who are needed at the various stages of making the vision happen.

From our earlier discussions, you will remember that 'attracting' opportunities is actually a matter of the mind's powerful filtering mechanisms being set so that we have the right opportunities brought to our attention out of all the millions of events that cross our paths every day.

It is exactly the same with people. Our minds will home in on the right people to take us where we want to be. Provided, that is, that we have set our minds properly in the first place and are prepared to listen to what they are telling us.

This mechanism is very powerful, so the best thing we can do is trust it to produce the results we want. We should avoid trying to improve its results by starting to plan things which are better off not being planned or force things which are better off not being forced.

The problem comes when we have specific candidates for some of these roles. If I decide for instance that the four clients have to be George W. Bush, Madonna, billionaire businessman Warren Buffet and the Prince of Wales, I am targeting my mind in a quite different way. Instead of being able to select from a wide range of possibilities it is now constricted to a limited field. If I fail to get those four particular people, I will register the vision as having failed, even though there are probably thousands of other people in the world who would have done just as well.

And what's more important, of those thousands there might well be some who are looking for just what I will be able to offer them. So that as well as their being part of my vision, I am part of their vision.

The degree to which you are able to influence or attract another human being depends almost entirely on how much their vision overlaps with your vision.

A *I've got a good example of this coming up at lunchtime today. I'm having lunch with another coach who I'm hoping will be part of the development of my vision. I've done a little bit of work with him before.*

Q So what are you going to do to make this go as well as possible?

A *I think according to what we have been saying I will go with no expectations and see it as a chance to share visions. I know he has a very strong vision of what he wants to do and this is a chance to see where his vision and mine overlap. And if they do, they do – and if they don't they don't.*

Q So you will be trusting your mind to make the most of any potential connections?

A *Yes, exactly.*

Q Let me know how you get on!

(later)

Q How did it go?

A *Not as well as I would have liked. I didn't really feel we were connecting somehow. But on the other hand he said he was willing to be kept informed. I think I'd have just liked a bit more enthusiasm on his part. So I was left feeling a bit let down and suddenly my vision seemed an awfully long way away. My confidence seemed to have vanished. I think by the time I got home I was thinking that all I wanted was a quiet life and why did I have to have all these big ideas?*

Q So what bits of the meeting did you feel went well?

A *Well, he did say that he was interested and I think he really meant it, and we arranged some other events that we were going to do together.*

Q If he were here now, how do you think he would say the meeting went?

A *I think he'd say that he was interested and would be waiting for some more concrete proposals. I think he would say he was reluctant to commit himself to anything without knowing more about exactly what was required of him.*

Q What would it take for you to be able to get his interest more fully?

A *He would like to have something definite to commit himself to.*

Q What do you think the likelihood is of being able to provide something he can respond favourably to?

A *Pretty high, I'd say. Assuming it works out at all, that is.*

Q So how are you feeling about the meeting now?

A *A lot better in fact. I can see it wasn't really the disaster I thought it was.*

Q OK. So what message do you think your feelings of it being a set-back were having for you?

A *Well, I think it was a useful reminder that I am not going to feel on top of the world the whole time. That discouragement is bound to come at times. And I think in spite of all I said beforehand I went into the meeting with too many expectations, and that in itself may have been picked up by him and made him react rather unenthusiastically.*

Q OK, what could you do to improve that next time you have a meeting like that?

A *Simply to share my vision the best I can. Once I have done that I have done my bit. Other people's reaction to it is up to them.*

Q So you would not be attached to the results of your sharing your vision?

A *No, the important thing is that I continue to share it. Talking of which it is time for another issue of my newsletter. And again I'd like to write about what we have been talking about, especially listening to what messages resistance and setbacks give.*

Welcoming problems as friends

One of the most deeply entrenched habits of mind that virtually everyone has is to regard problems as adversaries to be overcome. This means that we often seem to spend most of our time battling problems. In fact, as I mentioned last week the number of potential problems we have is virtually infinite. We can always find some more to fight.

I would like to propose that we look at problems in a radically different way – as friends to be welcomed.

Why? Because problems and setbacks are usually the times that we learn the most valuable lessons and make the greatest growth. If we had a world in which everything was perfect we would never learn anything and have no impetus to grow – we would also be bored to tears!

I have just had a very powerful demonstration of this, which I would like to share with you. I have been really struggling with my second book and finding it more and more difficult to write. I knew very well what the message was that I wanted to get over, but I was having a really hard time getting it down on paper. I was resisting writing and what I did succeed in writing seemed to be completely failing to get over the spirit and reality of what I wanted to convey.

I was battling and battling away at this problem, trying to find a way to overcome it. And then a week ago I realised that I was ignoring my own words in the book about treating problems as friends to be welcomed. What would happen if I treated this problem as a friend?

So I asked myself, 'If this resistance I am feeling to writing my book is in fact my mind giving me a strong message, what would that message be?'

The second I asked the question I realised that the reason I was resisting writing the book was because I was unhappy with the *way* I was writing it. I saw clearly that I wanted the book itself to be an example of everything that I was saying in the book. So it had to be written according to the principles I was teaching and had to show those principles at work in my own life at the same time.

So, with two months and eleven days to go to the deadline for delivery of the book, I decided to scrap everything I had written and start again!

This was a terrifying decision to make. But the effect of starting the book again from scratch and this time writing it the way I wanted to write it was like taking a cork out of a bottle. One week later I have written 26,814 words, just about half the total book! The effect of listening to what my resistance was saying instead of fighting it has been that I have written as much in seven days as I wrote in seven months before. A thirty-fold increase in productivity! And what's more I am extremely happy with what I have written.

Exercise
Choose a problem that you have been battling for some time without success. Instead of thinking of ways of overcoming it, ask yourself: 'If this problem is a friend with a message for me, what would that message be?' Then listen to the answer and be prepared to act on it!

Q I see the number of months you have been writing this book has gone up!

A *Well I've actually been trying to write it for about a year now so that would make it even more impressive.*

Q Anyway you've got over halfway through the book. And we've done over 2,500 words again today. That is a tremendous achievement.

Wednesday, 29 August – Changing our perspective

Q What's been better since we last spoke?

A *On the personal organisation side I had a real problem to find anything at all that was better when I wrote my list last night. In fact I sat there for what seemed like hours thinking, 'There must be something!'*

Q And did you find something in the end?

A *Yes, it was an interesting one. In the end I wrote, 'I didn't feel the need to force myself to be up to date with everything.' What I meant was that I can now trust myself to deal with my e-mail, tidying, etc. etc. when I feel like it and know it'll get done, but yesterday after a busy day I hadn't cleared everything and I started to feel as if I'd failed. So I was able to say to myself, 'It doesn't matter, it will get done when it needs to get done.'*

Q This was an *ought* trying to creep in by the back door – and you successfully dealt with it. Well done!

A *The other area that things were really better in yesterday was my weight. You remember we talked about how I didn't want to feel I was on a diet the whole time? Well, yesterday I found myself just naturally eating the right things. I didn't have to force myself or even think about it that much. It was especially impressive because I was out to lunch with someone, and that's always a time of extra temptation. So I have a real feeling that this isn't going to be a problem from now on.*

Q What's made the difference?

A *Well, it's all three parts of my methods working together. It's a very good example of how that happens. First of all I've got a clear vision:* I am in total health and look and feel younger than I did ten years previously – and am much fitter than I was then.

Q And I note the vision is in terms of health, which is a positive thing. It's not a case of just avoiding being fat.

A *Yes, that's right. So I am seeing my weight in terms of a larger vision of being totally healthy of which it is a part. Then I used the self-coaching to help me to pick out what was going right.*

Q So it got you away from seeing your weight as a problem and instead onto what was going well?

A *Yes, but I had to acknowledge how I was feeling about it first before I could do that.*

Q So acknowledging the Present Reality, including your feelings about it, is an essential starting point?

A *Yes. You have to be prepared to face up to the negative, not try to deny it. And lastly putting every new advance, however small, on the 'What's Better?' list seems to make the mind want more.*

Q So what's the total effect?

A *It seems to be to trigger that feeling we spoke about before. The feeling that one* knows *it's going to work this time. I've occasionally felt that before but I've never known how to produce it at will. Now I think I have learned how to.*

Q That really is something, isn't it? You are talking about methods that just about everybody needs.

A *Yes, and even for those people who don't go for these particular methods, they provide a starting point which will enable them to design something which will fit them better . . . And now I've got something I would like to talk over with you.*

Q Sure.

A *Someone e-mailed me in response to the newsletter I sent out last night about welcoming problems as friends. She said she'd had her car stolen with two files in it which she'd been working on for months and she'd got toothache which had resulted in three visits to the dentist. And* *generally she had so much on her plate that she felt as if she were trying to climb Mount Everest. So although she agreed with me intellectually, she was finding it very difficult to deal with what the newsletter said.*

Q Yes, I've always found that toothache is a wonderful way of bringing one back in touch with real life!

For there was never yet philosopher
That could endure the toothache patiently.

What has been good about this e-mail for you?

A *For me? I thought we were going to talk about her problems?*

Q You should know me better than that by now! I want to know what has been good about this e-mail for *you*.

A *Well, I think it's been useful to remind me that real people do have real problems in real life, and often they do get quite overwhelming.*

Q And?

A *And that we're talking about an ideal here, not something that can be kept to all the time. A change of mental attitude. We are not trying to deny the reality of problems. But it's our attitude to them that determines how they are going to affect us. If we can say, 'Where's the learning?' whenever we get a setback then we are going to keep advancing. It's like the difference between saying, 'If only I had done so-and-so,' and saying, 'Next time I will do so-and-so.'*

Q And?

A *Well, I suppose I could ask her to look at how she handled the experiences. Because she* has *survived them, she's still here, so she must have handled them somehow. And there may be important bits of recognition there which she can build on about her own resourcefulness in handling setbacks and emergencies.*

Q Great, so you would encourage her to find the bits which she did handle well?

A *Yes. And that would probably help her more than all my theorising!*

Q Yes, probably!

A *I think the really important thing is to see problems and setbacks in the context of one's Future Vision. To see them as part of the process of attaining the Future Vision. If you can do that it takes a lot of the sting out of them. And then you can look at them from the point of view of seeing how they are progressing you towards that vision.*

Q Can you give an example?

A *Yes, if you look at how discouraged I felt when I had lunch with my fellow coach yesterday. It made me look at the whole way I was putting over my vision, and reinforced the lesson that I shouldn't put expectations onto someone. In fact, it was a pretty good practical lesson in the theory I had been talking about just beforehand.*

Q And what would have happened if it had gone perfectly?

A *I'd probably have had a quite unrealistic feeling that nothing would ever go wrong again. And I would have had an even harder bump when that blew up in my face, as it inevitably would. I also wouldn't have learnt anything from it. And anyway where's the fun if everything goes perfectly the whole time?*

Q So in our relationships with other people we've seen how important it is not to load them with expectations. Because if we do that we are simply trying to impose *oughts* on them, when *oughts* are exactly what we are working at getting away from. And I think you are saying that relationships between people are always best based on a shared vision.

A *Yes.*

Q So I would like to ask you whether there are other methods of helping to align ourselves with another person?

A *There are two techniques I often use when I feel that I am out of alignment with someone. Neither of them are original to me. I've picked them up over the years and have found that they work for me. They are* *both writing exercises. One is an exercise in putting oneself in the other person's shoes. You pretend you are the other person and then write the answer to three questions: What am I thinking? What am I feeling? What do I want?*

Q Can you give an example of how that might work?

A *Yes, I used to do a lot of work with churches which needed to raise money for repairing their church building. Now there's a big tendency in fundraising to think that because you are a 'good cause' and you need the money other people* ought *to give to you. And it's very important to get people out of that way of thinking – fast! So I often used to give them that exercise to help to put them into the shoes of their potential donors. Otherwise they would sit around saying things like: 'Well they* ought *to realise how important this is,' or, 'They* oughtn't *to be so selfish.'*

Q I get the picture! So what sort of results would you get from the exercise?

A *Well let's try it, shall we? I'll role play being a member of a church fund-raising committee who is doing this exercise.*

Example – The church fundraising committee

The situation

St Agatha's intends to approach members of the local non-church-going community about giving to the restoration appeal for its beautiful historic church, which is the oldest building in the village. The members of the fundraising committee feel that the whole community *ought* to give to the appeal because they use the church when they feel like it, i.e. for weddings, baptisms and funerals, but never give it any support otherwise. They have approached members of the public on this basis but have had very little response.

The members of the committee have each been asked to imagine they are a non-churchgoing member of the community who has been sent the appeal letter from the committee. Now they are individually asked to write the answers to the three questions. A typical example of this exercise might go as follows:

What am I thinking?

I do appreciate the church being in the village and I'd miss it if it were knocked down or something, but I don't really see why I should be expected to pay for it. I mean it isn't as if I go to the church at all. I think it should be members of the congregation who pay for it. Most of them are pretty rich anyway. I know my daughter got married there about five years ago, but the way they go on about it you would think you have to pay for the privilege for ever. We did pay for it at the time and gave a donation. What more do they want? You don't find the village shop coming round and asking you to pay for evermore just because you bought a few things there once. I don't go to church myself but I don't have anything against people who do – but I think they should pay for the privilege themselves and not expect other people to fork out.

What am I feeling?

If I'm honest I'm feeling pretty upset to get a letter telling me that I should be giving to the church. If I give to something it will be because I want to give to it and not because someone is trying to make me feel guilty. I don't think they appreciate how tight things are these days.

What do I want?

What I'd like to know is a bit more about why they need to raise the money at all. What's it all for? If they explained that properly then I'm sure more people would be willing to give. And I'd like to be sure that the people who go to church have done their bit before they ask the rest of us. And come to that, what's the church ever done for us?

From all of which the committee members can become more aware that they need to:

1. Explain to people clearly why the money is needed.
2. Make a case for the church building being of interest to the whole village because it is an important historic monument and the focal centre of the village.
3. Show that the congregation has led the way by contributing themselves.
4. Make sure the church building is seen as a resource for the whole community and not just for churchgoers only.
5. In short, show people why they would *want* to give rather than why they *ought* to give.

This method is very useful in a wide variety of situations and can be used to get a different perspective on how both individuals and groups are thinking.

Q Thanks for explaining that. Now you said there was a second method which you use. What is that?

A *The second one is for use with individuals. If you are having difficulty relating to someone, then it's a good way of working through your own feelings about the situation. You can use it in relation to your close family, friends, your boss, colleagues, clients – anyone you might have a situation with that involves strong emotions.*

Q How does it work?

A *It's very simple. You write them a letter which you don't intend to send. The idea is to say everything you feel about the situation. Really be honest about your emotions. Once you've got it all out, good and bad, put the letter away in a drawer for twenty-four hours and then re-read it. And then decide whether you want to re-write it, send it as it is, or take some other action. Or simply decide to do nothing.*

Q So you are giving your mind a chance to cool down and get a calmer perspective?

A *Yes. There's a variation of this, in which after you've written your letter* *and put it away for twenty-four hours, you then write the other person's reply to your letter. That can be very illuminating if you want to understand things from the other person's point of view.*

Q So in dealing with other people, the secret is to look at things from their perspective?

A *Yes, it won't solve every possible problem of course. But an awful lot of conflicts could have been avoided if people had been able to step out from their own point of view. It's another case of the mind acting as a filter. If you have a particular point of view everything you see or hear tends to be interpreted to fit your point of view. You literally can't see anything that doesn't fit. But by changing your point of view you become aware of a whole load of things you hadn't been able to comprehend before.*

Q You are literally blind to them up to then?

A *There's an old military saying: 'If the enemy has two possible courses of action open to him, you can be sure he'll take the third.'*

Q Well, we've written another 2,500 words today, so it's time for bed!

Thursday, 30 August – Don't wait for the future to start living

Q **What was better yesterday?**

A *On the being well ordered front, I remembered to empty my briefcase when I came back from giving an evening workshop. And the other thing I remembered to do was to look at my tickler file first thing in the morning. These are only small things but they are important for efficient running.*

Q **That's excellent. So bit by bit you are getting more and more organised?**

A *Yes, and the important thing to remember is that I am doing all these things because I feel like doing them rather than because I am forcing myself to do them.*

Q **How does that work?**

A *It feels as if I simply can't stand being disorganised. When I see the office looking untidy, I want to clear it up. It's not an obsessive feeling. Just the feeling that I prefer to be tidy rather than untidy. So things get tidied up naturally, rather than being forced.*

Q **Since we started talking nine days ago how much have you been able to be well ordered in this natural way?**

A *A huge amount. There are still some areas which I haven't extended this to. One is getting my backlog of paper sorted out, and another is filing.*

Q **Which is the more pressing?**

A *The paper I think. I made the decision nine days ago when we started talking that I was not going to deal with any paperwork until I felt like doing it. Well so far I haven't felt like doing it. So I have accumulated a week's worth of paper. Which I hate. I want to get rid of it.*

Q So you are finding your mind is already more than half prepared to get rid of it.

A *Yes.*

Q OK, let's focus a little more closely on this paperwork. How did you get all the other things ordered in the way you wanted them to be?

A *I put them on the 'What's Better?' list because you told me to find something every day that was to do with being well ordered.*

Q Let's focus a little bit closer in then. I'd like you to find one thing each day that's better specifically about paperwork.

A *That's a good idea. And of course I've got Day One already, which was remembering to clear the papers out of my briefcase.*

Q That's it!

A *I can feel my attitude to paperwork changing already. Which makes me wonder whether one can use this method to break bad habits.*

Q Have you got a particular one in mind?

A *Yes, I've always had a problem with biting my nails. Do you think I could break it this way?*

Q Let's find out, shall we? First of all, is it part of your vision? Remember the first step is that whatever you want to achieve must be included in your vision.

A *Yes, I think it's there implicitly. The person inhabiting that castle isn't going to be the sort of person who has bitten fingernails!*

Q OK, that's good enough. As long as you can see it as part of the vision, it doesn't need to be spelled out.

A *What's the next step?*

Q Find something that's already better about how you bite your nails.

A *Umm . . . that's difficult. Let's see . . . the nail on my right middle finger looks better than any of the others. How's that?*

Q That's fine. How did it get to be better?

A *I think it's just because it looks better I tend to leave it that way.*

Q Good. Now find something to put about your nails on the 'What's Better?' list every day.

A *Right. You know something funny?*

Q No, tell me!

A *I'm finding that one of the effects of this dialogue is that I am beginning to think like you.*

Q That's interesting. How does that work?

A *Well, you are my Future Self, the person who inhabits my vision. So you are me after you have achieved my vision. In other words you are the person I am aiming to become.*

Q Yes?

A *I wrote something about this for my clients. I think it would be a good idea to put it in here.*

The present

One problem that many people have with goals for the future is that they see their goal as something that must happen before they are able really to start living. They forget that life is for living *now*. Of course a strong vision for the future does give purpose and direction to life in the present, but even so it is easy to allow your life to become something you will have in the future, rather than having it now. An example of this is the executive who has missed his children growing up because he has worked so hard to provide for his family – a classic case of missing the point of why he was working in the first place. I have used masculine pronouns to describe this executive because it used to be an almost exclusively male phenomenon, but nowadays it is making inroads into some women's lives as well. And generally speaking women are just as capable as men of putting their 'real lives' off until some mythical future date.

Another thing that many people forget is that their Future Vision may require them to be a very different person from what they are today. If I have a vision of myself in several years' time living a perfectly ordered life as I run my worldwide business empire and take instant decisions worth millions of pounds, what would really happen if disorganised indecisive old me was actually plonked down in the middle of that scenario?

The bad news is that I would need to be a very different person. The good news is that I don't have to wait till then to become that person. I can become that person right now in the present. And of course if I do, I don't just become the person running that business empire, I become the person who *built* that business empire.

Exercise

Take your vision for the future. Now imagine somebody who had actually achieved that goal. Picture what sort of person they would be and how they would look and act.

Now stand up and imitate that person's bodily posture. Move around a bit, take a few actions, and see how it feels. Then relax and go back to being 'yourself' again.

How different did you feel when you were pretending to be the other person? What did you feel when you went back to being yourself? Which person did you prefer being?

Could you switch back to being the other person if you wanted to?

One thing you may discover is that you don't like being the person you would have to be to achieve the goal. In the example of the business empire above, you may decide that you are not the sort of person who would ever be really happy in those circumstances. It sounds great to be rich and powerful, but do you really want the hassle and worry that goes with a position like that? The newspapers are full of stories of people who 'made it' as film stars, singers or whatever and were unable to handle the pressures that went with the job.

So one effect of feeling what it would be like to have your goal may be to realise that you don't really want it after all. In that case it is important to identify *why* you thought you wanted the goal and then see if you could get the benefits in some other way.

As an example of this, some time ago I set myself the goal of making a million dollars. I think I decided on a million dollars instead of pounds because it was a smaller amount of money but the round figure of one million seemed like a good thing to aim for at the time. Yet the very fact that I had chosen a round figure like that showed that I hadn't worked out what I wanted it *for*. It was just an arbitrary figure.

I soon found that the money itself didn't motivate me that much. So I then decided to look at what the idea of a million dollars really meant to me. I wrote down a list which went something like this:

- freedom from debt
- freedom to do what I want
- freedom from worry
- etc.

I realised that the reason I wanted money probably had something to do with freedom!

So did I have to wait until I had earned a million dollars before I could have freedom? Weren't there things I could achieve in the shorter term, or perhaps even immediately, which would have the same effect? I began to realise that the goal of a million dollars was in itself a burden. In order to reach freedom, I was proposing to enslave myself to a huge goal for an indefinite period of time. Surely there must be an easier way of doing things!

Once I had worked out the reason I wanted the money I was able to set myself goals which went to the heart of the matter. Within two years I had succeeded in freeing myself from all debt – I even paid off my mortgage early – and had resigned from my employment so that I could do what I really wanted. And what's more I had sufficient financial reserves to be free from worry.

So by concentrating on what the goal of $1 million really meant to me, I was able to get what I wanted much more quickly and directly.

Whether or not you already have a long-term vision of what you want your life to be in the future, spend some time working out what you want your life to be like *now*. You don't have to wait until you achieve your life vision to lead a perfect life. In fact if you do postpone living until some time in the future you won't be able to enjoy your big vision even when you do achieve it, because you won't have become the person to fit the vision.

Exercise

Use the Goal Achievement Method to write a goal about what you want your life to be like in the present. Use exactly the same method of writing the goal, i.e. in the present tense, using feelings, and describing what you do want not what you don't want. Here are a couple of examples of what you might write:

Example One:

My life is totally perfect in the present. I feel like a first-class traveller in life. I can get to wherever I want to be in the quickest, smoothest, most effective and enjoyable way possible. My goals for the perfect future are important to me, but it is the present where I live and work and have my being. And that present has a quality that is transforming. I feel that I am at the cutting edge of life. The way I live has a quality about it that is instantly perceptible. It is as if I can do everything and be everything that I want to be instantaneously just as an act of creation.

Example Two:
My life is fantastically spontaneous and purposeful because I have no resistance to what my mind is telling me is the right thing to do. I simply know what is the best thing to do next and do it, without even the slightest gap between hearing and starting to do. The result is that I live a life of absolute freedom and spontaneity, which at the same time is unbelievably well ordered. Because I am so sensitive to the inner workings of my mind I am incredibly intuitive and opportunities present themselves to me all the time.

You can use either of these as the basis for your own goal or write your own from scratch. Then, as before, write your Present Reality in relation to the goal. Don't forget to regularly edit the goal and write out the Present Reality.

Q That's very useful. What you seem to be saying is that, in order to achieve your vision, you already need to be the person and to live the life that that person would be living in the vision.

A *Yes, I realise that if I, as I am today, were suddenly plonked down in my castle, with a training institute to run and some very high-profile clients to deal with, I would never be able to survive the pressure. I need to find a new way of living. In other words I need to become* today *the person that my Future Self would be. And what's more I need to be living* today *in the way that he would live if he were transported back to here and now.*

Q So by imagining me (your Future Self) and dialoguing with me in this way, you say you are actually learning to think like me?

A *Yes, I'm finding it in all sorts of odd ways. Like how I'm much more willing to let things happen rather than push them, but at the same time I've become very much more aware of* how *things are moving me* *towards my vision. And that makes me very responsive when an opportunity arises. And my mind seems to pick up on growth, rather than getting bogged down in what's not working. Still a long way to go though!*

Q I think it's remarkable progress. And you are right, to achieve your vision you have to *be* the person in the vision. I found that out at a very early stage.

A *When was that?*

Q About now I think!

A *I'd like to tell you about something else that was better yesterday and reflects that.*

Q OK. Go ahead.

A *One of the problems I've been having is that as I've been developing the methods and living more and more in Pull Mode myself, I've become more and more dissatisfied with the way I've been putting over time management in seminars. Chiefly because most of what I was teaching was Push Mode stuff. Anyway, last night I gave an evening workshop for a group of small business owners, and instead of talking about what I usually have in the past I incorporated a lot of what we have been talking about. Things like the 'What's better?' list and having powerful goals.*

Q What sort of response did you get?

A *It went down really well. In fact one of the guys said at the end something on these lines. 'I really liked your different approach. You don't seem to use the standard time management stuff. Instead you're saying that if you have clear goals and you concentrate on growth areas and what you're really good at, and you make things easy for yourself by having good structures and systems, then time management will look after itself.'*

Q Sounds as if he got the message!

A *Yes, they were all very appreciative. And I was very glad I'd had that meeting because it means I've had the chance to try this approach out on quite a small audience before I get the big challenge of the workshops I'm doing for the major household name company.*

Q So once again it's worked out well without your having to plan it.

A *So it has! I've only just realised that. I couldn't have planned it better if I'd tried.*

Q You're always saying that . . . And by the way we've just achieved our 2,500 words for today and it's only 10.40 a.m. What are you doing for the rest of today?

A *I'm going up to London. Meeting someone for lunch who's a possible good contact. And then in the early evening there's a meeting of the London Coaching Group.*

Q So lots of possibilities there?

A *Yes, but I'm definitely going with no expectations this time!*

Q What can you do to make this meeting better than the last one?

A *Well, I think it will probably go better simply because this is really just a friendly meeting. I don't have any particular agenda to discuss with this person, unlike the last. So if anything comes out of the meeting it's a bonus.*

Q So you can just let it be?

A *Yes, that's a good way to put it – let it be whatever it turns out to be.*

Q Which is a pretty good way of looking at life itself?

A *Yes, but this is important – provided you are in Pull Mode and not Drift Mode. Otherwise you'll just be stagnating.*

Friday, 31 August — Acceptance

Q **What's been better since we last spoke?**

A *You asked me to look specifically at something to do with paperwork.*

Q **Yes.**

A *The truth is that I can't think of a single thing to do with paperwork that's better.*

Q **Not one?**

A *Well, I suppose I remembered to look at my tickler file yesterday and today. That's a definite improvement.*

Q **Anything else?**

A *I simply have been away from the office too much over the last two days to clear any paperwork. Nothing got touched.*

Q **Nothing at all? Or were there exceptions to that?**

A *The only one I can think of is that I made sure I had all the papers I needed for the meetings I had yesterday and today.*

Q **That's great. So even during two days in which you were hardly in your office at all you still managed to bring forward the papers that you needed without any trouble?**

A *Yes, I guess I did. And several backlogs have built up over these two days but I am confident that I will clear them tomorrow without any fuss.*

Q **That's good. What else has been better?**

A *One thing interested me a lot yesterday, and that was that during the evening meeting I had a lot of very mixed emotions. I think it was all to do with my big vision. And anything that anyone said or did which seemed to have anything which might possibly jeopardise the vision made me feel really peculiar.*

Q Can you give me an example of that?

A *Well, any mention of people doing similar things, particularly if they were more advanced at it than me. It was almost as if I was jealous of what they had achieved. So that was a very negative sort of emotion, and frankly I was surprised by it. I thought I had risen above feelings like that!*

Q Were there times when you felt better than that?

A *Oh, yes. I had one moment during the day of pure blessing. A friend of mine gave me a present, a completely unexpected one, and I suddenly felt really uplifted by it.*

Q I get the impression that you were surprised by how you had all these emotions going on at the same time, positive and negative.

A *Yes, it was quite a kaleidoscope, no doubt about that.*

Q So if these emotions were your mind trying to tell you something, what would that message be?

A *I think it was the same thing I was complaining about the other day. I am too attached to things working out in a certain way. Instead of letting my mind find the best way to my vision, I keep trying to tell it what it should be doing. But then suddenly I get a reminder that I need to let things happen. I should say that the person who gave me the unexpected present was the one with whom I had that rather unsatisfactory meeting the other day. At least I saw it as unsatisfactory. But he may well have a completely different perspective on it.*

Q So you seem to be saying that instead of letting that meeting happen the way it happened, you were judging it?

A *Yes, if I hadn't been judging it, it would have been much easier – for me anyway.*

Q So judgement seems to be one of the ways that Push Mode manifests itself?

A *Yes, in Push Mode we are always telling the world that it's not the way we want it to be. If we can let things change rather than try to make them change we will not always be struggling against life as it actually is.*

Q So how do we ourselves fit into this if we are not trying to change things?

A *We are letting ourselves change too.*

Q Can you give me a practical example?

A *Yes, a very simple example is the tidiness of my desk. I haven't had time to tidy it over the last two days, so it's got a bit messy. Now I can if I want judge it as a bad desk, and judge myself as bad for letting it become a bad desk.*

Q Which doesn't sound very productive.

A *No, because it probably means I will resent having to tidy the desk, so it won't get done. But the other attitude is to accept the desk as it is and accept myself as I am, and at the same time be prepared to accept that it may change into a tidy desk and that I may change so I play my part in that. And if I have a strong vision of a tidy desk, then we probably will change in that way but only when we are ready to.*

Q There's a third way of course, which is simply not to care whether the desk is tidy or not.

A *Yes, that's Drift Mode.*

Q This habit of judging can be very ingrained, can't it?

A *Yes, we do it all the time. For instance when I have a public speaking engagement, I know that just about every single member of my audience will have made about twenty judgements about me before I've even started to speak.*

Q Really? Is it as bad as that?

A *If you don't believe me, try a little exercise. Next time you find yourself sitting somewhere where there are quite a number of other people – like* *in a restaurant, or a railway carriage or whatever – listen to what you are saying to yourself about the people. You'll find you've got this stream of thoughts going on, that goes something like this: 'She's fat – why doesn't she go on a diet', 'Why's he wearing that hideous tie?', 'I can't stand people who play loud music through earphones', 'What a strange looking person', 'Why do they have to talk so loud?' There'll be some positive judgements but most of them will be negative. And you'll find that just about every time you look at any other person, there's a thought like that which goes with the look.*

Q Isn't this fairly harmless?

A *Not really, because every one of those thoughts is preventing us from accepting the person as they are. Every one of those examples I gave just now is saying that the person* ought *to be different. It's bad enough when it's just random strangers, but we do this to the people we meet every day as well. And after a while we keep having the same thoughts about them and become unable to see them in any other way.*

Q And we do this to things as well as people?

A *Yes. If I look at my desk now, I am thinking, 'That paper's untidy', 'Those cups need clearing away', 'I must put my keys in the right place', etc. etc. In other words, my desk* ought *to be different!*

Q So what's the answer?

A *I'm now going to look at my desk and say, 'It's fine the way it is, and if it's going to change in any way that's fine too.'*

Q OK . . . Hey, what just happened there?

A *I tidied the paper, cleared away the cups, and put my keys in the right place!*

Q So once you'd accepted it the way it was, you found you had removed the block to its changing?

A *Yes.*

Q That's amazing!

A *There's one aspect of this that's really important for us to look at, and that's to do with the past. The thoughts we've had about people in the past can imprison us in the present.*

Q I'll bet this is where you produce one of those articles you've written for your clients.

A *How did you guess?*

The past

I hope by now that you are well practised at using the Goal Achievement Method for attaining goals that lie in the future. The method can be used for goals that lie in the short term, medium term and long term. I shall be returning to the subject of future goals in a later module. For the time being you have enough information to continue to work in the future.

I want now to turn to a different subject – the past. When we think of goals we naturally think that they are intended to affect the future, but an interesting and very powerful use of my method is to affect the past.

It's not possible of course to change the actual events of the past, but what we can change is our attitude to the past and our interpretation of it.

It is our attitude to the past that determines how it is going to affect us in the present. If there are many things in our past that are unacknowledged or unassimilated, then we are going to continue to find that our lives continue to be negatively impacted by them. If on the other hand we have fully accepted and integrated our past we are freed to build on it. Essentially our past is a 'given', something that however positive or negative it was at the time only has as much power to affect the way we act in the present as we are allowing it.

The exercises I am going to give now are not designed to deal with deep trauma in the past – that is the role of therapy – but to help people relate better to the ordinary ups and downs of life. There are two particular ways in which the past can affect us that I want to deal with now.

- Lack of forgiveness.
- Negative patterns.

Forgiveness

Let's deal with forgiveness first. The inability to forgive people is one of the most crippling ways in which we can allow the past to have a negative hold on us. We need to be clear that it is primarily us who are negatively affected, not the person whom we are not forgiving. By forgiveness we can free ourselves from the negative influence of the other person.

Exercise

Draw up a list of everyone in your life you haven't forgiven for something. This is one of those lists that can be as long as you like. It doesn't matter if the thing you need to forgive is something big or something small, whether it is an isolated incident or a whole relationship extending over many years – perhaps even over your entire life. Write them all down – big and small. However small the resentment, it is having an effect on you in the present.

And don't forget to put your own name on the list – often we need to forgive ourselves even more than we need to forgive other people.

When you have made the list as complete as you can, go down it one name at a time and say to each person, 'I forgive you.' You don't have to do more than say the words.

With some people this will be easy. With others the words may bring a flood of emotion. With yet others the words may be impossible to say. Don't worry if this is the case – just go on to the next name on the list. When you have completed the list, go back through the people you were unable to forgive on the first pass and see if you can say the words. You may find it easier this time.

If there are still some people you have been unable to say, 'I forgive you' to, then see if there is some neutral attribute of theirs which you can say the words about. For instance say, 'I forgive you for the colour of your hair' – but don't pick this if the colour of their hair is what irritated you most about them!

This is an exercise which can be repeated over the next few days. Each time you go through the list your forgiveness of the people on it will get deeper and deeper. You will probably also think of additional names to go on the list.

Negative patterns

One of the ways the past keeps its hold over us is by keeping us to habitual patterns that may have been useful in specific situations in our history but are having a negative effect now. A pattern represents the path of least resistance. We have gone that way so often in the past that the path is worn deep and it is easier to go down it rather than strike out into new territory. The way to overcome a negative path is to establish another path in its place – hopefully one this time that will have a positive effect.

The key to achieving this is 'Do one thing different'. Once you have recognised that you have a problem with a negative pattern, then look closely at what you are doing. You will nearly always find that you follow a familiar sequence of events. If you can do just one thing in the sequence different, then the pattern will be broken.

Example:

You have a problem with incoming paper not getting actioned and ending up in piles. If you look closely at what is happening you see that it invariably follows the same pattern. You look at your mail, open each envelope in turn, look at the contents and put them in a pile. You then don't have time to go through the pile and it subsequently gets the next day's mail added to it, making it even less likely that you will have time to deal with the pile.

Notice that you can break this pattern at any point in the sequence. Here are some suggestions:

- Don't open your mail at all – throw it all directly into the waste paper basket. You won't succeed in actioning things any better, but at least you won't have any piles! Seriously this sort of shock tactic can be very effective in breaking a pattern – you won't want to keep it up for very long of course, but it can make you re-evaluate your whole attitude to mail.
- Open your mail one envelope at a time spread throughout the day – and action it directly. Don't open more than one envelope at a time.
- Open your mail in one go, action anything that you estimate will take less than two minutes and decide *when* you are going to action each individual item that will take over two minutes.

Exercise

Identify a negative pattern in your life. Whenever you find yourself complaining about something or someone and using the word 'always' or 'never', you are almost certainly describing a negative pattern – 'I can never catch up with the paperwork', 'They always leave their rooms in a mess', 'I can never stick to a diet', 'He always forgets our anniversary'. When the pattern involves another person, either person has the power to break the pattern by doing something different.

- Look carefully at what happens. What sets off the first step in the sequence? What is the next step? And the next? What happens as a result?
- Take each step in the sequence in turn and decide at least one thing you could do differently at that step.

- Choose *one* of the different things you have come up with and start doing it. Make a conscious effort to do it in place of the existing pattern until it becomes second nature.

Making a goal about your past

Acceptance of your past is vital if you are going to be able to live fully effectively in the present. So let's use the Goal Achievement Method to change your attitude to the past. Write it using exactly the same techniques that you would use to write a future goal – using the present tense, describing feelings and only describing what you do want. Here is an example of what a goal like this might look like:

> *My perfect past*
> I know that everything that has led up to this moment in my life has been a perfect preparation, and so has every action that I have ever taken. I rejoice at how it has all fitted me exactly for the life I am choosing and the wonderful things I am creating. I see how not a single bit of knowledge or experience has been wasted. I realise that every person I have ever been in contact with has played their part too and I am thankful that each one has brought exactly the gift that I needed at that stage of my journey. I am at peace with my past, accept it joyfully and delight in how free I am to express myself now and in the future.

Exercise

Write out your own goal for your own perfect past. Use your own words rather than copying mine.

And now treat it in exactly the same way that you would treat a future goal. Write it out and revise it daily to start off with, and write a paragraph describing your Present Reality each time.

Saturday, 1 September – Becoming one's Future

Self

Q What's been better since we last spoke?

A *I had a really weird day yesterday. I had to get up early for a breakfast meeting, having hardly slept at all that night. And then I was away for the morning and lunchtime visiting a management college. I got stuck in unusually heavy traffic on the way back and had to keep stopping because I kept feeling sleepy. So a journey that took me two hours going took me four and a half coming back. I missed one client appointment as a result, and had quite a few important calls waiting for me which it was too late to do anything about. And today I felt so tired that I stayed in bed until nearly lunch-time – which is very unusual for me. So I've got that feeling that I have done absolutely nothing for nearly a day and a half.*

Q So was everything uniformly bad?

A *No, far from it. For a start the two meetings I had, the breakfast meeting and the management college, went very well. And in spite of being very tired last night, I was absolutely determined to keep writing the book.*

Q So something you were resisting less than two weeks ago, you now can hardly stop yourself from doing even when you are exhausted?

A *Yes, that's extraordinary.*

Q What would you say is your number one priority at the moment?

A *No doubt at all – writing the book.*

Q So even on a day as difficult as yesterday, your feelings ensured that you did what was most important?

A *Yes, that's interesting. I really hadn't seen that. I was looking at all the things that didn't get done. But none of them are anything like as* *important as the book. In fact, what my feelings seem to have said was, 'Forget about all the other stuff – just get on with the book.' And it's interesting that today what my feelings seem to have gone for is first to ensure that I got adequate rest and then that I got on with the book again.*

Q So your feelings are actually protecting your most important current activity from all the other trivia that is being chucked at you?

A *Yes, that is just incredible. I simply hadn't realised that that was what was happening until you made me look at it.*

Q There's something radical happening here. Instead of the Push Mode consciousness which says, 'you *ought* to have done this, you *ought* to have done that', you are learning the Pull Mode consciousness which enables you to respond as needed to what you are perceiving.

A *Yes, but until you made me look at what was happening I still had the Push Mode type voices making me feel guilty, even though my* actions *were Pull Mode actions.*

Q That's a huge advance you've made, because what happens to most people is that when they can't keep up with what Push Mode is telling them, they fall into Drift Mode instead and just goof off.

A *So how can I get rid of this Push Mode thinking altogether? I would be a lot happier without it I think!*

Q Have there been times when you have felt reasonably free of Push Mode thinking?

A *Yes, like when we first started on this book twelve days ago, I just refused to do anything until I felt like doing it. And some stuff got done and some didn't but I was trusting my mind to know what to do and when.*

Q And how did that work out?

A *Well, the big fear was that everything would just pile up and I'd spend my whole time slumped in front of the TV. But in fact that never happened. I found that bit by bit I was getting my life into a better ordered state than before. But also that I knew when to let go of that when necessary.*

Q What were you doing to make that work out like that?

A *I think I was really trusting my feelings to find the best way through everything. And because I had made a definite commitment that I would follow them even if it ended in disaster – that I would accept that as a possibility and it was OK – that commitment seemed to shut off the Push Mode thinking somehow.*

Q And what message has yesterday got for you?

A *Well, it was like a demonstration that I* can *trust my feelings to look after what really matters. I can even trust them when I have all sorts of voices telling me otherwise. And I've just realised something.*

Q What's that?

A *It's like we talked about yesterday – that you can disarm something by accepting its right to be as it is and also its right to change. So what if I were able to say to the Push Mode voices 'You're fine the way you are, and if you change in any way that's fine too'?*

Q Try it and see!

A *OK, I'm saying to all my* oughts *I appreciate what you are trying to do, and I'm grateful for the contribution you've made to my life so far, and you are just fine the way you are. And I shall appreciate you just as much if you change in any way that you want to change.*

Q How do you feel now you've said that?

A *It's very odd. It's almost as if I've set my Push Mode thoughts free to change into something better.*

Q I think it's time now to try something which we've talked about before. We've done the basic dialogue that we are engaged in

now, your Present Self talking to your Future Self. And I hope we've demonstrated the value of that as a regular, daily practice. But what I'd like us to try now is to make a further leap of the imagination and to play a dialogue between your Future Self and *his* Future Self.

A *Yes, that should prove very instructive. The point of the dialoguing we have been doing up to now has been to look at what I am up to in the present from the point of view of the future. The point of this new dialogue is to expand my vision for the future and make it more powerful. That in its turn will of course affect what I am doing in the present.*

Q I have suggested that we do it now, rather than right at the end of the book, because it may raise important issues that need to be part of the agenda of the rest of the book.

A *How do we run this?*

Q We'll keep the basic Q and A dialogue. But in this case your Future Self will be A. And his Future Self will be Q. We'll call them AF and QF to avoid confusion with our normal dialogue.

A *So this is me imagining you imagining yourself talking to your imaginary Future Self?*

Q Yes.

A *Well, that's totally clear then!*

Role play – Mark's Future Self (AF) being coached by his Future Self (QF)

QF So how are you getting on coaching young Present Reality?

AF *It's fun. It brings back what it was like when all these things were new to me. The thrill of discovery and the excitement of realising that they really worked.*

QF **And have you turned out the way he was expecting and hoping in those days?**

AF *Oh, very much so I think. But what I have come to realise is that what really matters is not the outward trappings, the castle and the training institute and the devoted followers and the money and all that. What really matters is becoming the person who created all that.*

QF **And now you are the person who created all that, how are you different from Mark as he was then?**

AF *Oh, I'm much less worried about what people think about me, or even what I think about myself. I just enjoy being. And creating.*

QF **Creating seems very important to you. What's so special about creating?**

AF *I think that's what we were created for. Created to create. Creating is what we are all about. But now I just enjoy the act of creating. What I create is less important to me. It's as if I were an artist painting a picture. I could paint anything I liked. But this time I pick a particular subject, say a self-portrait. And the next time I do a landscape. Or the other way round, it doesn't matter. Whichever feels right at the time.*

QF **How else are you different from him?**

AF *I don't like preaching as much as he does. He's filled this book with methods and teachings, but I prefer teaching people by example and by encouraging them to learn by experience.*

QF **And are you still using the methods he describes?**

AF *He asked me that, and he thought the answer would be yes. But in fact it's no. But the reasons are interesting.*

QF **Well, let's look at them one by one. Do you still use his Goal Achievement Method for your life vision?**

AF *I still have a clear vision of what I want to achieve and I am still very honest with myself with where I am with respect to it. And I* *still use my feelings as the motivator and the guide to getting there. But what's different is that the subject of the vision itself becomes less and less important to me. It's the process of creating it that is the whole point. Just like a painter loves the process of creating a painting, but once it's created he moves on.*

QF **So basically it's the same process he describes but you have internalised it more.**

AF *Yes, but there is another difference which is that when he designed his vision he was thinking in terms of three to five years in the future. But now I have visions that are much closer than that. In fact they are often quite near in time.*

QF **Is that because you are able to manifest them quicker?**

AF *Yes, definitely. I have much less in the way of mental baggage getting in the way.*

QF **And what about the 'What's Better?' list?**

AF *I don't use that, but the reason is because I have learned to realise that everything that happens to me is better.*

QF **How does that work?**

AF *Whatever my initial reaction to something is, good or bad, I quickly realise that I am judging it, and instead I look to see how it is taking me towards the vision. It may seem to be a setback, but it will be teaching some lesson or strengthening some mental muscle (or sometimes even a physical muscle) that I need.*

QF **And what about this dialogue? Are you still using that?**

AF *Yes, but it's much more of a way of discussing issues with myself than a coaching session. Your coaching style with me is different from the style that I used with him. That's because you don't need to be continually affirming me or getting me to look at what's been going well. That's the natural way I think anyway. So you are more of a sounding board. Also you are much more similar to me than I am to him.*

QF So the main difference seems to be that you have internalised the methods so that they represent much more the way you think, rather than an artificial writing exercise?

AF *Yes.*

QF Now I'm interested that you said that the main point of the vision is becoming the person who created it. And he said not long ago that he thought he was beginning to think like you.

AF *Yes, he is already beginning to change noticeably.*

QF Now I am going to suggest something – tell me what you think about it.

AF *OK.*

QF I think the time has come for you to stop coaching him, and instead for me to start coaching you as if you were living his life every day.

AF *So that he really does start thinking like me?*

QF So that, at least during this dialogue, he is living as though he were the person he wants to become.

AF *I think that's a great idea. It would be a different slant. Instead of being asked questions about his life from the perspective of his Future Self, he would be looking at his life directly through the eyes of his Future Self – and learning directly how to think like that person.*

QF And another thing that this new perspective will bring is that all the teaching in this book so far has been from his perspective in his Present Reality. But something we can discuss is what teaching we can bring from the perspective of the future.

AF *I know one thing I would really like to see is an essay from each of us giving the truth about why we wrote this book.*

QF How do you mean?

AF *I mean I would like Mark's Present Self to write an article called 'The Truth About Why I Wrote This Book' and I will then write one myself on the same subject.*

QF **And perhaps I might write one as well.**

AF *The contrasts and the similarities might be very interesting.*

QF **What other subjects do you think we might cover?**

AF *I think we will find that the subjects we need to cover will arise naturally.*

QF **This is a good point to finish this role play, because I think you need to talk to Mark's Present Self to make sure he is happy about being done out of a job.**

Q **What did you make of that?**

A *I thought it was brilliant. It took me completely by surprise, but the idea of thinking about my life as if I were you sounds just like what I am ready for.*

Q **Good. So I suggest that we finish for today now, and tomorrow we will resume with QF and AF.**

A *Yes, that's great. In the meantime I can write that section you two were talking about –* 'The Truth About Why I Wrote This Book'. *I remember Brad Blanton wrote a similar piece in his book* Radical Honesty. *I'm not sure I'm prepared to be quite as radically honest as he was, but anyway here goes!*

The truth about why I wrote this book

I wrote this book for a whole variety of reasons, most of which are not ones which I am very comfortable admitting. But this is an important exercise for me and it is important for the development of this book. So let's get it over and done with.

I suppose the number one reason was because I wanted the sheer pleasure of being someone who has written a book – no, even better, I will now be someone who has written two books and had them published. That immediately puts me into a class above most of the people I know. And it is a really wonderful feeling having people congratulate me on getting published. And it is an even better feeling when they write to me and ask me how to do it. And the best feeling of all is when they write to me and tell me what a difference the book has made to their lives. And I like that not so much because I have made them feel good but because their thanks and admiration make me feel good.

And I have written the book because I like to think that I might make lots of money out of it, and because it might lead to giving seminars and talks and a jet-setting lifestyle (never mind that I hate flying).

And another reason I have written it is because I can tell all my friends that I am writing another book and describe all the ideas I am going to put into it. And tell them that if they need any help writing their books then I am very happy to advise.

And I enjoy the bustle of talking to editors and publicists and agents and appearing on the radio and reading reviews. It all makes me feel wonderfully important.

And I have written the book because it concentrates my mind on the subject and makes me work things out for myself. And then other people will think how brilliant I am.

Sunday, 2 September – Self validation

QF **That's an interesting little piece Mark wrote there. Just goes to show that our motives are not always what they appear to be.**

AF *But of course other people sense what they are even if they too collude in hiding them. I'll write my own version of the reasons for writing this book in a moment. But first, it's Sunday which is our day for formally updating our Present Reality.*

The vision

No change.

Present Reality update

I have now written a total of 37,886 words in twelve days, an average of 3,157 words a day. This means I have kept up the same rate of writing that I reported in last Sunday's Present Reality. If I keep this rate up I should have finished the book by the end of this week

I have continued to follow my feelings and among the things that have changed as a result I have now stopped biting my nails, and I feel far more confident about maintaining my weight at the desired level.

I ran a successful seminar last week which has made me feel much more at ease about what to present at the series of seminars I have this month.

During the week I have made some useful contacts who may be significant for the future.

I have fixed up a telephone conference call at the end of September on the subject of 'Setting Powerful Goals', but I am having nightmares about whether I am going to get any attendees or not. If I don't get anyone it will destroy my plans for running a series of classes through the medium of telephone conference calls.

QF **It sounds as if Mark has had another powerful week. How do you think you are going to compare?**

AF *Well it's interesting taking over in this sort of way, because one of the first things that happens is that you can feel all the shoulds and oughts rising up out of their graves and it's a bit like a scene from a horror film. They all started advancing on me with their arms outstretched muttering, 'Future Self has taken over. Everything is going to be perfect from now on. We're going to get everything done as it ought to be at last.'*

QF **Ha! I'll bet you disillusioned them pretty quickly.**

AF *I certainly did. I didn't take the slightest bit of notice of any of them. I spent the day basically doing nothing, except a few odd jobs like mowing the lawn. And now I'm writing the book, but that's because I want to not because I ought to.*

QF **That's a big difference?**

AF *It certainly is. There's all the difference in the world between doing something because you want to do it and doing it because you feel you ought to do it.*

QF **So did you feel you wanted to mow the lawn?**

AF *Not exactly; what I wanted was to have a garden that looks good. And when I do eventually tidy my office it won't be because I like tidying but because I want a well ordered office.*

QF **And eating well is because you want to be healthy?**

AF *Exactly.*

QF **So how do you manage to prioritise among all these activities?**

AF *That's Push Mode talk. I don't prioritise at all. I rely on my mind to know when it's time to do something and what to do.*

QF So is that what happened today?

AF *Yes, you'll remember last Sunday exactly the same thing happened, except that Mark wasn't as relaxed about it as I am. I know that my mind will make sure that I get adequate rest, provided I don't slip back into listening to all the oughts and shoulds.*

QF So what do you do when an *ought* comes screaming up to you?

AF *I simply say 'My mind will tell me exactly the best possible time to deal with you – which may be never!'*

QF I'm really looking forward to hearing why you wrote this book. Perhaps now would be a good time to do that?

AF *Yes, OK. This should be an interesting exercise.*

The truth about why Future Self wrote this book

I wrote this book for a very clear and definite reason – because I wanted to. I wanted to because it was an act of creation, an expression of where I am and who I am. And to me the important thing is not who reads it or what their reaction is but the fact that I wrote it and that I see it and it is good.

I hope that other people will enjoy it and find it interesting, but if they don't that is fine by me. Once it is finished my life and my interest will pass on to other things. I will enjoy talking about it and hearing about its effect on people, but that is not the reason I wrote it.

It may be a book that is different from what anyone else has written before, but for me the important thing is that it is different from anything that *I* have done before. It has stretched me and developed me and made me think. And it has used everything that I have inside me at the moment to produce it. It is my creation and once it is finished I will send it out into the world to make its own way. It will go with my blessing, but I will let it go.

QF I am amazed. There seems to be no relationship at all between your two 'Truths'. Which one is the real you?

AF *You hardly need to ask that do you? The difference between them is obvious. The version by Present Self is all about how he gets his motivation and validations from outside himself, from other people's reactions or external things like money or lifestyle.*

QF And yours is all about your own internal validation of yourself.

AF *That's right. And the danger for Present Self is that if he's getting his validity from outside, then he will collapse if the outside validation disappears for any reason.*

QF So learning to think like you is going to involve a complete change in the way he validates his experience? But in doing that he will find his real self.

AF *That's right!*

QF Now excuse me for mentioning this, but there was one thing I noticed that was missing from *both* of your 'Truths'.

AF *What was that?*

QF Neither of you made any mention of having written the book in order to help other people. That sort of surprises me. Perhaps not with Present Self so much because it's not surprising that his motivation is up the creek. But somehow I expected you to put something in about being 'dedicated to the future welfare of humankind' or that sort of thing. After all you're supposed to be some sort of Higher Self, aren't you? And aren't Higher Selves supposed to be dedicated to that sort of higher mission?

AF *First of all I am not a Higher Self. I am Mark as he imagines he will be in the future. And the difference between him now and him in the future is only the difference between external and internal validation. I'm still the same self. By imagining me as he wants to be he is beginning to learn to think like me.*

QF OK, so what about the higher mission?

AF *What could be a higher mission than to give people a demonstration of how to be creators of their own lives?*

QF Yes, but what about demonstrating to people how to cooperate with each other and help each other?

AF *There are some very important points that need to be made about this. So I think this is a good time to write at more length.*

One's own best interests

If we need our lives to be integrated, then what is the guiding principle that we should follow which will give that integrity – which will stop us being at war with ourselves?

I would suggest that it is *to act always in our own best interests.* This is a very difficult concept for most people to deal with. Most of us are brought up to think of acting in our own best interests as selfish. By the word 'selfish' they mean a mean-spirited, ungenerous attitude which grabs what it wants at the expense of other people and doesn't care less what other people think or feel. In fact this is the very reverse of acting in one's own best interests, since it can hardly be thought to be in anyone's best interests to alienate other people so that they will not cooperate.

The results of confusing acting in one's own best interests with a narrow mean-spiritedness are disastrous. In the effort not to appear 'selfish' people often become completely cut off from their own wants and desires. And since it is very difficult to give what one doesn't have, they become insensitive to the wants and desires of those who are close to them too.

Another result of this confusion is to cut people off from reality. As children we are usually discouraged from exploring what our own best interests really are in favour of conforming to other people's vision of what we should be doing. This usually means that instead of doing what we really believe is best for us we end up either doing what other people want us to do or rebelling against it, neither of which brings us any nearer to following our own vision for our lives.

At its most basic the brain is an instrument for achieving the best interests of the organism. The higher the organism the more sophisticated the brain and the more sophisticated the strategies it follows. However, this sophisticated functioning will revert to lower levels of functioning when faced with contradictions it cannot resolve.

The message that is given to us when we are young and that comes over loud and clear is that what is in our best interests is not in our best interests. Faced with having to integrate the contradictions implicit in a message such as this the brain tends to close down whole areas of experience.

Let us look at how someone would act who follows their own best interests consistently. People who act consistently in their own best interests would be likely to:

- be clear about what is important in their lives and pursue those things single-mindedly;
- cooperate with others to achieve results;
- look after their own health and fitness;
- refuse to engage in self-destructive behaviours;
- select their friends carefully and maintain those friendships;
- stay in touch with the reality of situations;
- refuse to take on commitments that are not consistent with their own vision;
- continually expand their comfort zones;
- ensure that they have the education and training to do what is important to them;
- build on the experience and wisdom of other people;

- be prepared to pay the price for what they want;
- regard the selection of a life partner as the single most important decision they will probably ever make;
- keep everything in their lives well maintained;
- be sensitive to their own feelings and needs;
- be aware of the likely consequences of their actions;
- think about long-term results rather than short-term ones.

This list is illustrative rather than exhaustive. But if we contrast the above behaviours with their opposites we can see more clearly how common it is for people not to act in their own best interests. People who don't act in their own best interests may:

- have no clear vision for what they want to achieve;
- see themselves in competition with other people;
- be overweight, unfit or otherwise not be taking care of their health;
- have self-destructive behaviours such as drug-taking, self-sabotage, workaholism etc.;
- neglect their friendships;
- do anything rather than face up to the reality of situations;
- be loaded with commitments that they resent;
- be stuck in a rut;
- fail to keep learning, either formally or informally;
- be reluctant to ask other people for help;
- not be prepared to put in the effort or cost needed to achieve what they want;
- select a life partner on the basis of the whim of the moment;
- live poorly maintained lives which are constantly in a state of crisis or breakdown;
- be anaesthetised to their own feelings and needs;
- ignore the likely consequences of their actions or lack of action;
- think purely in terms of short-term advantage.

So we can see that far from being 'selfish' in the pejorative sense of the word, acting in our own best interests results in highly desirable behaviour both from our own point of view and the point of view of other people. In fact an accusation that someone who is acting in their own best interests is 'selfish' usually means that the accuser wants the 'selfish' person to sacrifice himself or herself for the accuser's benefit.

Again I would stress the point that what we think of as typically selfish behaviour, such as grabbing everything for oneself at the expense of other people, is hardly ever in one's own best interests. But the way to discourage such behaviour is not to teach children that they should sacrifice their own interests for the interests of others, but to show them why this type of behaviour is not really in their interests at all.

Exercise

Ask yourself the question: 'If I were consistently to act in my own best interests, what would I do differently?' List as many things as you can, both large and small. These are some of the items, out of a very long list, which one of my clients wrote in answer to this question:

- I would only say yes when I was able to say it wholeheartedly, otherwise I would say no.
- I would go to bed at a sensible time every night except for special occasions.
- I would make time to spend on my own.
- I would stop putting off the decision to change jobs.
- I would stop shouting at my children.
- I would make it a priority to get out of debt.
- I would stop leaving the choice of holiday up to my partner.
- I would stop bringing work home in the evenings.
- I would plan a family outing at least once a month.
- I would check the car tyre pressures regularly.
- I would face up to my financial position.
- I would work out why I keep losing vital bits of paper.

We can use this concept of enlightened self-interest as a tool to evaluate potential courses of action. Perhaps even more important we can use it as a tool to evaluate our current actions. I will use the word 'self-ish' with a hyphen in this context to distinguish it from the pejorative, narrow use of the word 'selfish'. Is what I am doing at this precise moment properly self-ish (in the sense of being in my own best interest)?

What I am doing at this precise moment is writing this paragraph, which is part of my goal of writing this book, which is part of my wider vision of where I wish to go in my life. So yes, what I am doing at this precise moment is indeed properly self-ish. But note that although my primary motivation for doing it is my own self-interest it is none the less an action which will (I hope) benefit other people as well. There is nothing anti-social or malevolent about being self-ish.

It has often been pointed out by theologians that the biblical injunction is 'Love thy neighbour as thyself', not 'Love thy neighbour more than thyself' or 'Love thy neighbour instead of thyself'. In fact logically it would be impossible for everyone to love their neighbour instead of themselves because who would do the receiving if that were the case? It would be like the scene in *Father Ted* where two women come to blows because each one insists that she should pay for tea. However, the idea that we should love other people more than or instead of ourselves is one that is very prevalent in our culture. And since it is a logically untenable position which it is actually impossible to keep to, it results in either guilt, denial or rebellion.

So one of the most important thing we can do in our lives is to give them integrity and unity by having one guiding principle to follow. And the best guiding principle to have is the enlightened pursuit of our own best interests.

QF I thought you said you didn't like preaching! But I think you are making the point very strongly that the behaviour of a

person who is self-validating is going to benefit humankind even though benefiting humankind was not his or her object.

AF *That's right. Attempts to sacrifice one's own interests for the sake of humankind are externally referenced actions which will have negative effects, both for oneself and for the people one is claiming to be helping.*

QF Such as?

AF *Such as creating a dependency culture for instance. And very often it involves imposing a whole load of* oughts *on the supposedly grateful recipients. Which quickly leads to resentment on both sides.*

QF Well, I think we can stop there for today. You've got a lot on tomorrow. I'm looking forward to seeing how Future Self handles it all.

AF *You don't get away as easily as that. You've forgotten you said that you too would write a piece on the truth about why you wrote this book.*

QF So I did! I hoped *you*'d forgotten.

The truth about why Future Self's Future Self wrote this book

My contribution to this book has been relatively small compared to the contributions of the other two. And what I have to contribute is perhaps only a slightly different perspective.

For me creation is all. But creation is not something that I carry out on my own. I have myriads of helpers and co-agents. They join in creating with me, sometimes for a second, sometimes for a lifetime and beyond. Some I hardly take notice of, indeed some I never meet. Some I am conscious of every moment of every day. We do not work for each other. We work with each other.

This book is not the work of one human being. It is the work of thousands upon thousands. As is every book. And each one has put their own individual stamp on it. Each one has shared a moment of their own vision.

No one has made us work together. We create because we want to. Because it is our nature.

AF *I had no idea you were going to write anything like that.*

QF **Neither had I until I wrote it.**

AF 'Who is he that hideth counsel without knowledge? Therefore have I uttered that I understood not; things too wonderful for me, which I knew not.'

Monday, 3 September – Life as a work of art

QF How are you getting on today?

AF *I started the way I meant to go on by getting up early and clearing various backlogs. I hit them hard and will keep on doing so.*

QF Can you tell me what the difference is here between doing this in Push Mode and doing it in Pull Mode? What you are talking about sounds very similar to how someone might work in Push Mode. Somehow I think of Pull Mode as being a whole lot more relaxed.

AF *It's a mistake to think that. One can be working very intensely indeed in Pull Mode. The difference is in where the energy is coming from. It's like I said yesterday, there is all the difference in the world between clearing backlogs because I feel I* ought *to and clearing them because I* want *to. I am powered by the vision I have of a well-ordered working environment. If anything doesn't fit that vision, then I am determined to get it out of the way. And I love the feeling of being on top of things.*

QF But yesterday you basically didn't do anything.

AF *That's right. Because I was doing what feels right. And on Sunday my unconscious mind was telling me through my feelings that I needed to rest. The one thing that it did keep me at though was writing this book.*

QF And I notice that even in the midst of your determination to clear backlogs, you are still writing!

AF *Yes. If I were in Push Mode I would probably be using the busy work of clearing backlogs to avoid doing the hard work of writing the book. But in Pull Mode I can trust my feelings to keep me in the right balance.*

QF Talking about balance, I was impressed yesterday by our three different versions of 'The Truth About Why I Have Written This Book'.

AF *Yes, I was too. Especially as none of us had the faintest idea what we were going to write. But the one I found most impressive was Present Self's.*

QF **Why was that?**

AF *Because he told the truth. Usually when you read what people say about what their aims were in writing a book, they proceed to give all sorts of bullshit about how they want to help people, etc., etc. I'm not saying they are necessarily insincere when they say that, it's just that they always have loads of hidden agendas as well. Which they often are not admitting even to themselves.*

QF **And that doesn't just apply to writing books, I suppose?**

AF *No, indeed.*

QF **Still, I would be interested to know what the 'official' reasons are for writing this book – the sort of things that go into most books' introductions.**

AF *So you'd like me to write the book's introduction for you?*

QF **Yes, I think that would be worth doing.**

The official Introduction to this book

Waste of lives

One of the most distressing things that can happen to a person is that sudden sense that they have not achieved anything like what they are capable of achieving – or believe themselves to be capable of achieving. And often at the same time comes the realisation that something radical is going to have to change if the rest of life is not to fall short as well.

This feeling affects most people at some time in their lives. It is a sense that the years are passing and we still haven't quite discovered what makes life tick. We feel that there must be something more, that we are somehow spread out over the surface of life but have not yet experienced its depth. We struggle perhaps for a while and then give up, resigned to the fact that our most impossible dreams are going to remain just that – impossible. As the French author and cynic Anatole France wrote: 'The vast majority of people want another life that lasts forever when they don't know what to do with the one they have.'

And yet – deep within us we still have those impossible yearnings. And they remain impossible so often because we are unable to articulate them – they are, in truth, more feelings than concrete aspirations. Most people would find it difficult to answer the question, 'What do you really want?' Any answers that we try to give to the question seem incomplete or contradictory or make us feel guilty. And most people have had the experience of getting something they thought they really wanted only to find that it brings no real satisfaction.

It has probably been like this through most of history. Yet the problem seems to have intensified in modern times. In the old days impossible dreams very likely *were* impossible. The limits of travel and society and technology confined the vast majority of humankind within very narrow boundaries. Yet for those who did break out the world was full of discovery and adventure.

Today, advances in technology have enormously increased our horizons. The courses open to the average person have been gigantically increased. And yet we seem to be no nearer our impossible dreams. The result of an increased number of possible choices has been that many of us have chosen too many things, so instead of experiencing a few things in depth we skate over the surface of a huge number of things. It is as if we had gone into a restaurant and ordered every item on the menu.

At the beginning of the third millennium humanity finds itself faced with a paradox. The circumstances of our lives have been revolutionised by huge increases in technology and show every sign of continuing to be revolutionised at ever increasing speed into the future.

I think of myself as a schoolboy in the late 1950s and early 1960s.

When I try to think back to myself as I lived then I realise that my life now would be complete science fiction to him. What is more, it would be completely unforeseen science fiction. As I glance around my office as I am sitting here writing I see many things that would have amazed him – my computer, the Internet, my mobile phone, my scanner, my fax, my colour printer. Even the humble calculator was far in the future as I struggled with the joys of long division using pounds, shillings and pence.

My earlier self might have been almost as amazed by the things that have not happened – that I am not now taking my holidays on the moon, that I am still driving a car with an internal combustion engine, that I still buy a cup of coffee with a dirty bit of paper and am given lumps of metal to make up the difference in value.

There is no reason to suppose that today's schoolchildren would be any better than I was at predicting their lives in thirty or forty years' time. We cannot even imagine the directions in which technology is going to take us in the future. We can be certain of only one thing – our lives will be very different from today.

But the paradox is that our circumstances are very different as a result of this new technology, but we ourselves are relatively unchanged. We still have the same minds, and very often the same mindsets, that humans have had for millennia. As individual persons we have not really caught up with the technology that we ourselves have produced. In fact what has often happened is that instead of liberating us it has overwhelmed us. Our world has been shrunk, our lives have been speeded up – and the result is we are unable to cope. The frantic pace of life stops us being balanced and takes the depth out of our experience. It is true that there are many more experiences to be had for the average person, but somehow we seem to live them in a shallower and shallower way. We could almost say that our minds are unable to deal with the world we have created.

What is more, our new technologies have provided no answers to the eternal questions that humans have been asking throughout recorded history: 'Who am I? Where am I going? What is it all about?' There are plenty of answers to these questions given by a multitude of sages and gurus. Unfortunately the answers are often contradictory and all are unverifiable. This book is going to make no attempt to answer these questions. Its aims are more modest and concentrate on the practical concerns of how, at the start of the new millennium, we can experience the fullness of everything that life has to offer. How in short we can live more deeply, more happily, more truly and more intensely.

To live more *deeply*? The experience of most people in our technological civilisations is that we live increasingly on the surface of life. Life is in danger of becoming a spectator sport. We live vicariously through the stars of sport, films, television and popular music. We are restless and driven, travelling further and further to find places that are becoming increasingly the same as they respond to the influx of tourists and modern life. As adults we complain increasingly about the short attention span of today's youth, while filling our own lives with such frantic activity that we can never pay adequate attention to anything. We have become more self-centred but have found that our selves have no centre. We feel as if we lack a dimension – as if we are two dimensional instead of three dimensional.

To live more *happily*? Happiness these days is increasingly seen as a feeling that we have no control over, rather than the natural result of a life well lived. Nowhere is this seen more tellingly than in the field of personal relationships where love is no longer seen as a decision and a commitment. Once the feeling is gone, the relationship is over. The old social concept of marriage as a contract in which both parties undertook to love each other as a *duty* is all but gone. We have got the cart before the horse. Instead of putting our principles and vision first, and making our feelings subservient to them, we have enthroned feelings as the prime cause of our actions. And by doing so we have surrendered control of our lives to every passing whim. It is not surprising that we are unable to build happiness on such a base.

To live more *truly*? Commitment and conviction are never allowed to get in the way of the impulse of the moment. Our personal preferences are rooted in nothing more substantial than immediate gratification. We long to be true to ourselves but lack the reference points to enable us to achieve this. The modern world has cast off the certainties of the past, only to discover that freedom without boundaries is no freedom at all. How can we be true to ourselves when most of us have no coherent answer to the question, 'What do I really want?'

To live more *intensely*? There is so much choice on offer that most of us are glutted on choice. The only way most of us can bring intensity back into our lives is to become hooked on adrenalin – the high that rush and hurry and speed and dangerous sports (of all kinds) bring. It is a dangerous high because it is addictive and can wreak havoc with our health and sense of being at peace with ourselves. But the sort of intensity that someone like Michelangelo or Edison brought to their lives, with their records of amazing and lasting achievement, is entirely strange to us. And the intensity of their lives did not arise out of a vacuum. They were the finest exemplars of ages in which society as a whole was in a ferment of artistic or scientific intensity.

This book is an attempt to find how we can indeed live deeply, happily, truly, intensely and how we can express our true selves with integrity and harmony.

This book is above all a response to Anatole France's saying that we do not know what to do with the life we have. It is an exploration of what to do with that life – the only one we do have.

In my first book, *Get Everything Done and Still Have Time to Play* I described my own struggles to find methods of managing time successfully and how, as a result of finding that the existing advice did not work for me, I developed my own methods. This book again is born out of my struggles with achieving goals and the lack of advice that works for me. There seem to be hundreds of books about how to achieve your goals. All of them I have found either don't work or are too much like hard work. But along the way I did discover some things that worked and began to put them together. And I found methods that worked for me and for many others.

What intrigued me more than anything was how some goals would come about in spite of there being no plan. Four years ago I made three very clear decisions. I decided that I wanted to be a writer; I decided that I wanted to be a great life coach; and I decided that I wanted to solve the time management problems that had plagued me all my life. When I formulated these decisions there was actually no connection between them in my mind. Three and a half years later I was a published author of a book on time management and I had a flourishing full-time practice specialising in coaching self-employed people in personal organisation. But when people asked me how I did this I could only reply, 'I didn't plan it – it just happened.'

Of course when I say it 'just happened' I don't mean there was no work involved. I mean that the opportunities seemed to arise out of nowhere, and so did the energy to carry them out. I was conscious that if I had planned them I could never have got them to happen the way they did.

It was as if the decisions I had made had drawn me to them, that making the decisions had opened my mind to the many opportunities around me and had even in some way attracted them to me.

I was fascinated by how this had happened – against every bit of advice that I had read about how to plan. It had all seemed so effortless somehow. As though all the trouble and worry of planning and carrying out a plan were unnecessary. The biggest change in my life had come about without my needing to worry about it.

It wouldn't be true to say that I didn't plan during this period. In fact I had loads of plans. But most of my plans didn't work or became too much effort. In the meantime the goals seemed to get achieved in spite of the collapse of my plans. Which of course raised the question – could I have saved myself a lot of effort by not trying to plan in the first place? If that was the case it would take a major burden off my life.

What I needed to do, I decided, was to learn how to reproduce this process so I could use it at will and also refine it so that its rather hit-and-miss nature would become more reliable.

Through my work with my clients, I had also learned that most people have very little idea of what they want. In fact many people have extreme trouble answering the question 'What do you really want?' I became convinced that one of the reasons people found it difficult to achieve goals was because they either never succeeded in formulating any real goals at all or because the goals they did formulate were not what they really wanted. Subconsciously therefore their minds were rebelling against them.

So as well as needing to refine the way of achieving what we want to achieve, I also set out to find a way in which I (and others) could refine what our goals are until they are really what we want.

What I wanted above all was to find a way of letting my life unfold. Of trusting my mind to take me where I wanted to be without the need for special techniques or conscious vigilance. I wanted, in short, to be able to relax and let it happen.

So the first thing I did was to make a conscious decision to let go of all the techniques in my first book. The result at first was a resumption of chaos. But gradually I began to find that the chaos was starting to decrease and things were beginning to happen in my life that were very exciting.

This is a very personal book because my own life has been evolving according to the principles contained in it while I have been writing it. In fact this book itself is a result of following these principles. At one stage I had 150 people actively trying out the Goal Methods I talk about, and the two case studies I give come from participants in this.

Exercise

This exercise is in two parts:

- Think back ten years and compare your life then with your life now. List some of the ways in which your life is different now. Which of these were the result of deliberate planning on your part and which 'just happened'?
- Imagine yourself ten years ago and write out what you would have liked your life to be in ten years' time, i.e. today. How different is it from how your life actually is today? If you really had written this out ten years ago, what decisions would you have taken differently from

those you did take? (Remember, doing nothing is a decision in itself).

- If your life today is exactly as you would have wished it to be ten years ago then you don't need this book. Perhaps you even *did* write out what you wanted in ten years' time and it has come to pass. But if like most of us you have a wide discrepancy or find it difficult to imagine what you would have wanted ten years ago then don't despair. You can learn how to maximise your likelihood of being exactly where you want to be in the next ten years time. Read on!

QF Deeply, happily, truly and intensely?

AF *Yes.*

QF Tell me, do you think that living more deeply, happily, truly and intensely is *better*?

AF *Yes, I do.*

QF If we think of some of the great characters in Shakespeare's plays, how much did they live up to this? Was Othello happy? Was Falstaff deep? Was MacBeth true? Was Hamlet intensely productive?

AF *Um, I'm not quite sure what you are getting at.*

QF Well, earlier on in this book there was some talk about how people preferred Dante's *Inferno* to his *Paradiso* and Milton's *Paradise Lost* to his *Paradise Regained.*

AF *Er . . . yes?*

QF And great drama uses the failings of the characters to make the play.

AF *I think I see what you mean. That people's failings are as valid as their successes?*

QF We've talked about how we see creation as being the really important thing, what we are designed to do. Now if we look at someone's life as a creation, then who are we to judge it?

AF *Yes, I understand now. So some of the most powerful plays and novels are based on the failings and frailties of their characters. And some of the most powerful paintings I know are of people and events which could hardly be called successes.*

QF So if someone comes to us and describes their life, we might say: 'What a fantastic creation. Look at this bit here, you have put in some real joy and love. And then what a contrast, frustration and despair here. And I love the struggle you've put in this bit. Wow, this angry bit is incredible, how did you do that?'

AF *It's life as a work of art.*

QF Yes, and what is important is that every work of art is perfect. It's their creation. It works for them.

AF *So if you were coaching someone, you might say: 'I love the struggle you've put in this bit. Tell me, how do you intend to develop that theme? Make more of it or fade it out?'*

QF You might not quite put it like that but, yes, that would be the general idea.

AF *I've noticed that when you're coaching me, it's much more like a general conversation. Yet I suspected that there was more to it.*

QF I like to take the attitude when coaching that we are two creators discussing their creations. And we'd be sharing our experiences, and seeing how we produce certain effects and how we are thinking of developing them.

AF *So you are saying that, whatever the person's life is like, they have created it as an act of deliberate creation?*

QF Yes, using the circumstances. Just as someone might go out into the garden and use the flowers they find there for a flower arrangement.

AF *And I think what you are also saying is that this creation of theirs works for them?*

QF Yes, otherwise they would have left it behind. So someone might create this marvellous story of the employee who can't summon up the courage to leave her job. But it's just a story. They could just as easily have created the story of the employee who leaves her job and triumphs, or leaves her job and falls flat on her face. But the first story is just fine. Lots of pathos and exploration of feelings, and a wonderful sense of nostalgia and yearning. Great literature!

AF *But what about people who have very restricted circumstances? How do they do this creation thing?*

QF Hasn't some of the world's greatest art been produced from very constricted forms? Think of the haiku or the sonnet or Jane Austen's novels.

AF *Hmmm. You're really making me think here.*

QF Well, look at your own vision of the future. In what way could you say that it's *better* than what you have now? It's different, that's all.

AF *I'm coming to the conclusion that you shouldn't really be coaching me at all. I'm only an imaginary figure. Perhaps you should be directly coaching Mark's Present Reality.*

QF Yes, that's fine. Let's be clear what's happening here. By using the method of dialoguing with himself in the future, Mark is succeeding in refining the best ways of using the methods for himself. That is to say he has used the initial methods to design a method that fits him even better for the stage he has got to.

AF *Let's start this dialogue up again then, with you and Mark's Present Reality. Are you going to keep on calling yourself QF?*

QF Yes, I think so.

QF Hi, Mark. You've got some fantastic stuff going on here. I think the way the book is being produced is really incredible. Talk about life as a work of art. And I love the struggles you keep having with personal organisation. How are you going to develop that?

A *I think it's about time I got rid of that personal organisation theme. It's getting a bit boring now.*

QF It's worked extremely well for you up to now. How do you see yourself moving on from it?

A *Yes, it's played a brilliant role in my life up to now. I've written a book about it, and then I had a big drama about throwing over the principles in my book and living without them. And I've even managed to base quite a big bit of this book on it too. So it's served its purpose well. But I think it's time to find some new themes and just let this one drop.*

QF What would you like to develop now?

A *I want to create something out of this business proposal which I've been contacted about. And of course, I want to get this book finally finished.*

QF Finally? A month and three weeks before the delivery date?

A *Yes, but my focus isn't on the delivery date, it's on getting the book out into the world.*

QF I'd like to give you my coaching principles before we really get going, because I think it's important you are clear where I am coming from.

Coaching principles

Life as a work of art

1. Your present life is your creation.
2. Your present creation works for you perfectly.
3. The only question is what you are going to create next.
4. Your next creation won't be better than your present creation, just different from it.
5. As a fellow creator, I love discussing the ways we create.
6. My creations are not better than your creations.

Tuesday, 4 September – Creation

QF What have you been creating today?

A *An interesting picture, full of contrasts and peculiarities!*

QF Tell me about them.

A *Oh, many themes intertwined. I created quite a bit of muddle in my office, and was fairly relaxed about it. In fact I spent the entire day sort of never quite getting round to having a big sort out. So I'd made a bit of uneasiness there. But it was balanced by some big advances in getting seminars going and in getting the coaching services business going. So there was a lot going on.*

QF Where did you feel the energy was today?

A *It was weird actually. I had a really deep talk with my wife last night about some issues, in which we were both entirely honest about our feelings. And that was incredibly liberating. I think we both felt the truth of the saying* 'the truth shall set you free'. *That is the truth about how we felt. Things which somehow get hidden and covered over. But the sense of freedom that came after we talked was amazing.*

QF Where did that come from?

A *I think one thing that this dialoguing does is make one very aware of what the truth is. And to desire truth perhaps more than anything else. What is speaking the truth other than being free to express oneself completely? Life is usually full of lies.*

QF So you gain power from speaking the truth?

A *Yes, tremendous power.*

QF Where is that truth going to take you?

A *I don't know. But I know that from now on I am going to be much more careful than I have been to avoid the sort of covering up of the truth that we all do every day.*

QF How does this connect with the rest of what you have created today?

A *I have to tell the truth to myself too, I guess. Admit that I am disorganised, that I am not an expert, that I have fears about being no good as a coach, that I worry about what people think about me. That I am far from perfect in short.*

QF That sounds an interesting creation.

A *I've created a powerful front for myself. And now all I want to do is to smash it up and come out and be real.*

QF And that really will be something. I love the determination you are putting into that. When someone can break through into reality like that and express it, it is a wonderful thing.

A *But I'm conscious of not being entirely honest even when I say all that. I may say I want to smash all this front up. But I suspect I will make sure that I will keep the bits that really matter.*

QF Tell me how that works for you.

A *Yes, the struggle is a phoney struggle of course. It's just an excuse. There's no struggle really. I can just step out and be myself if I wish to be so.*

QF If you decide that that is your next step of creation.

A *Yes, if I decide. I have the freedom not to decide too.*

QF They are both wonderful. If it works for you, keep it. Or at least until you want to change it. Masks are fun. There's nothing necessarily better about living without a mask. It's just a different way of living.

A *But I think I want to see what it's like. To experiment.*

QF Great! I love experiments!

A *Or perhaps I'll write a piece about this guy who keeps saying he wants to come out from behind the mask and peeks out and then shoots* *back in behind it again. Do you think that would be a good piece to write?*

QF **It would be fascinating to see how you did that.**

A *I would put in lots of feelings of frustration and fear and load myself up with chains, which I would say were unbreakable.*

QF **And they are really made of cardboard?**

A *How did you guess? Perhaps you should be writing this.*

QF **I have my own plays to write. I am writing one at the moment about 'Life As A Work of Art', and we are both characters in it.**

A *But the thing I really, really liked about today was the contrast between all the things I'd promised myself that I'd do today and what I actually succeeded in doing.*

QF **Contrast makes good art.**

A *And I've been looking at this really untidy desk I have and thinking, 'I created that!'*

QF **What techniques did you use to create it?**

A *It's easy. In fact it's just as easy to create an untidy desk as it is to create a tidy one. You just reverse the technique. Instead of putting paper where it's supposed to be, you put it in a random position on your desk. And the same with all the other bits and pieces.*

QF **As easy as that? I must try it sometime!**

A *Yes, it really works well. And then once the desk is untidy it allows you to throw in some frills like saying you are never able to find anything.*

QF **Yes, those make nice artistic touches.**

A *But I could never be as good as some people at this. I knew someone once who had ten years' worth of papers in his office, completely unsorted.*

QF **That is incredible. He should give lessons.**

A *I think he did. It worked fantastically well for him. It meant he never had to do anything on time and he had a perfect excuse for everything that went wrong.*

QF **When you look at genius like that it makes your own humble efforts look somehow inadequate.**

A *Yes, but I don't think I'm even going to make the effort to imitate him. I'm going to try a bit of variation. I'm going to go back to putting the paper where it's supposed to be for a bit.*

QF **Hmm. If you say so. Sounds a bit insipid to me. But it's your creation.**

A *I'll experiment. I want to see where the energy goes to anyway.*

QF **Where are you feeling that energy is leading?**

A *That's just it. I really don't know. I want to follow it wherever it goes.*

QF **Where's that energy coming from?**

A *It's just the feeling of being a creator. That I can make anything I want. No, that's not right. Because there's a sense in which the thing created makes itself. I don't know how or why it got there. All I know is that I made it and it expresses me.*

QF **It's not got much to do with tidy offices, has it?**

A *No! But then there's a voice inside me saying that untidiness is just a phoney excuse. An act. To get at the real energy, to make the real creation, it's necessary to drop the act.*

QF **Back to the truth again?**

A *Yes.*

QF **What is the truth about this, then?**

A *The truth is that I have needed untidiness and disorganisation to* *hold down my energy. So I've provided it. When I really let my energy go, then we will see some creation.*

QF **And where will truth lead you?**

A *To recover myself. And then to produce a magnificent work of creation. So much greater than all the petty work I have done up to now.*

QF **I'm looking forward to seeing it.**

A *One other thing I found today. I found myself getting in touch with my body again. I listened to what my body was saying about what it wanted to eat. And I did some exercises. A sort of mixture of yoga and Pilates and just free-form stuff. I felt great afterwards.*

QF **That's another theme that you are incorporating. Tell me, one thing I would like to know is do you still feel that your vision is the same, or do you want to change it?**

A *Not at the moment. I think I see that as an almost arbitrary thing. But then every work of art is arbitrary. The artist could have chosen another subject. But he chooses this one, rather than that one. So the change I feel is that I am no longer imprisoned by my own vision. I have chosen it freely, and I can lay it aside again freely if I wish to.*

QF **That's a big change?**

A *Yes, it's another step into freedom. Not becoming a prisoner of my own message. And I've realised something else.*

QF **Yes?**

A *That you've taken me further in twenty-four hours than I have gone in the whole of the rest of this book.*

QF **How did that happen?**

A *The way you coach is liberating. I feel as if I have been set free from all the guilt and frustration and heartache that I felt, because you have somehow validated everything that I've done. It's weird but seeing every creation I make as working perfectly puts me right at the centre of my own universe. Does that make sense?*

QF **Perfect sense.**

A *And I am amazed at how this dialoguing process has produced this. It has led me unerringly to finding out what I feel I really needed to know. And anyone can use this to find their own truth.*

QF **That is your creation – a gift to the world.**

A *Yes, not a sacrifice – a gift.*

QF **We've reached the end of our creation for today.**

A *Thank you.*

Wednesday, 5 September – Trusting the process

QF **We've talked about creation and seeing where the energy of our creation is leading us. Where have you felt the energy of creation today?**

A *I've done a lot today. But one thing I have been holding back on is really catching up with all the backlogs. It is a feeling as if I am holding back. But I know that I have done the things that really count. I have talked things over with my publisher, who is delighted with the way the book is going; I have heard from my agent that a national paper wants to interview me for an article about my time management methods; I have taken the business venture further forward; I have been preparing for the series of seminars over the next two weeks; I have interviewed a couple of potential clients; I have been asked to do a follow-up seminar following the success of the one last Wednesday; I have written several important e-mails to colleagues; I had a very useful coaching session with my own coach; and finally I finished work early and went off to the cinema with my wife.*

QF **It doesn't sound to me as if you have been holding back at all!**

A *Actually the list does sound rather impressive written out like that. But nevertheless I have been feeling all day that I have been holding back on getting really up-to-date.*

QF **That implies that you feel that you *could* have caught up if you had wanted to.**

A *Yes, I could if I had just had that little bit more determination to do it.*

QF **You do rather amuse me at times. You make your struggle to get organised sound like some sort of cosmic battle on which the fate of the universe hangs.**

A *But that is exactly what it is. The fate of* my *universe hangs on it. The vision I am creating includes being perfectly organised. So, perfectly organised I have to be!*

QF Nevertheless today's creation is perfect too. So how is what you have created today the precursor of your vision?

A *Today's creation is perfect too? Yes, of course. So what is perfect about this difficulty I am having – how is it working towards my vision?*

QF Yes.

A *It can only mean that the things I have done today are more important for me to be doing at this time than being perfectly organised.*

QF How does that work?

A *So, learning not to be too busy, to take things at the pace my mind tells me is right for me, not to push myself, to respond to things that I perceive as important, to be prepared to let things happen, to avoid getting hung up on inessentials, to communicate with colleagues and friends, to take time to take my wife out – you think these might be more important than having the paper cleared in my in-tray?*

QF Unlikely . . . but possible, yes.

A *So it's a question of learning what is really important?*

QF And more than that.

A *If I didn't have some disorganisation in my life, I wouldn't learn the lesson about what is really important?*

QF Go on.

A *So once I've learned that lesson, it's possible that the disorganisation will fall away because I don't have a need for it any longer?*

QF It's possible. How else might this be working for you?

A *I saw yesterday that I had been using disorganisation as a damper on my energy. Now I'm seeing that my mind is using it to teach me what is really important. So does this mean that once I see what is really important I will get the energy that I have been damping?*

QF How would that work?

A *Just trusting the process. Trusting that my mind will know exactly what is important to do and when.*

QF **You've been here before.**

A *I have. But I have to keep coming back to it because each time I learn more about having faith in my own mind. And the more I trust the process the less I worry and the less I feel that I* ought *to be doing something other than what I actually am doing at any particular moment.*

QF **Tell me how this affects the writing of this book.**

A *I knew last night that my mind was telling me not to worry that I hadn't written so many words as I had written up to now. And I feel I want to stop now for today and not attempt to write more. And I also think my mind is telling me to make this coming Sunday the last day of this dialogue – for the book that is, because of course I will be continuing it for myself alone. And then I can do the final editing over the next couple of weeks. And get the book in to the publisher by the end of the month.*

QF **And strangely enough your publisher asked you today if you could get the book in before the scheduled date, and here you are in a position to get it in a month early.**

A *Yes, strange how these things work out.*

QF **You said it! What will you do in the final editing process?**

A *I don't want to alter these dialogues because the whole point is that they are a genuine record of what has happened. So I will confine myself to making sure they make sense. But what I do think is necessary is to add a descriptive heading to each day, and add a summary at the end of each day too. And I might add some more exercises and case studies. And write a foreword. I guess that would be about it.*

QF **Fine! And I think that's enough creating for today.**

Thursday, 6 September – Space

QF **Tell me about today's creating.**

A *Today has been completely different. I took the day off and drove down to the West Country with my wife to her godmother's ninetieth birthday party. We had a good time catching up with friends and family. I have done no work today except for sending a few e-mails. I listened to my feelings and they said to put everything on hold today.*

QF **Where does that fit into your vision?**

A *To have space in my life – that is an essential part of my vision. To be able to take time to do what I want and enjoy the present. And this evening I listened to some music I like, and of course am writing this. But I'm not going to write much tonight.*

QF **Where will you go next?**

A *I know what I am feeling about tomorrow and the day after. I feel it would be right to create something completely special on those two days, which will be the last I write up in full for this book. Something incredible. So I am going to show this process of creation by giving a detailed record of my feelings and what I do as a result of them. And we will see the power that that can bring!*

QF **You sound very confident.**

A *Yes, because I feel it is right to do that. And I have learned to trust my feelings. Those two days are different from each other because tomorrow (Friday) I have several things in my diary. And on Saturday I have nothing at all scheduled. So we will see in detail how Pull Mode deals with those two scenarios.*

QF **What do you have in your schedule for tomorrow?**

A *It goes like this:*

06.45 Business breakfast meeting (2 hours)
09.30 Three-way conference call with associate coaches (open-ended)

12.30 Coaching client (40 minutes)
15.00 Coaching client (40 minutes)
18.00 Coaching client (40 minutes)

QF So this will be a creation round fixed points, while Saturday will be a creation on a totally empty canvas?

A *That's right.*

QF And what are these special things you are going to create on those two days?

A *I don't know yet! That's the fun of it. All I know is that they will in some way form part of my overall vision.*

QF Why are you so sure of that?

A *Because the book is essential to the completion of my vision, and I know my mind intends to produce a grand finale to the book. And I am certain my mind won't let me down.*

QF This is fascinating. I can't wait to see what happens. By the way, aren't you supposed to be producing your weekly newsletter today, or was it yesterday?

A *Yes, but I don't feel it's right to produce it yet. So I don't intend to until I do feel it's the right time.*

QF Till tomorrow then.

A *Yes, good night!*

Friday, 7 September – Transcending the vision

QF Tell me about today's creation.

A *Here is what happened in detail throughout the day. When I wrote the diary section in my first book,* Get Everything Done and Still Have Time to Play, *I was using the principle of doing what I was resisting the most. Here I am doing what I feel like. The results strangely enough are surprisingly similar. The real difference is that now I am acting under the direct influence of a strong vision. In fact, today's work was more effective because my feelings led me unerringly to what was most important for the vision. This is as much a record of my feelings as of my actions.*

Detailed description of Friday, 7 September

To get to my breakfast meeting I had to get up at 6 a.m. And although I was tempted to stay in bed, I found that I wanted to get up. I have in fact been wondering for some time whether to continue to belong to the networking organisation that runs these meetings, but my feeling at the moment is that I should continue to belong for the time being. This is a case of simply trusting one's feelings to tell one when it is the right time to leave. So, as I have said, my feeling this morning was that I should honour the commitment and that overruled my reluctance to get up.

I was back home from the meeting just before 9 a.m. and spent a few minutes opening the mail (all except one item was junk) and scanning the newspaper headlines. I did the washing up, checked my e-mail and then got ready for the three-way telephone conference call with my two fellow coaches who are associated with me in setting up an initiative to coach clergy. We had a good meeting for an hour and a half. The interesting thing was that when we first started talking about this six months ago we all needed clients. Since then all three of us have been doing very well and our lack of urgency on getting this initiative going has been more due to having no need for it than anything else. We decided however that it would be good to move forward now, because the lack of pressure meant that we could do things the way we each individually wanted to do them.

The meeting was over just before 11 a.m. and I spent the next forty-five minutes dealing with my e-mail. Following my feelings led me to sign on for a business breakfast event in London at the end of the month, which one of my contacts is running. It sounded like it would be a good opportunity to meet some creative people. Someone else had sent me a long video file, so while it was downloading I felt it was a good time to cut the garden hedge.

I then remembered that I had promised myself to re-subscribe to the *Harvard Business Review* and I spent some time finding their web site and signing on on-line. By now it was time to prepare for my 12.30 p.m. client. After I had finished the session with her, I had lunch and read Walt Whitman's *Passage to India.* The last two verses particularly struck me:

> Sail forth! – steer for the deep waters only,
> Reckless O soul, exploring, I with thee, and thou with me,
> For we are bound where mariner has not yet dared to go,
> And we will risk the ship, ourselves and all.
>
> O my brave soul!
> O farther farther sail!
> O daring joy, but safe! are they not all the seas of God?
> O farther, farther, farther sail!

So far today I had followed my feelings in everything. What this basically means is that I did what I felt like doing. I didn't ask myself what I felt like doing, I just did it. Every now and then a thought would cross my mind that I *ought* to be doing something or that something *needed* to be done, but I would dismiss it by saying to myself, 'I'll do that when I feel like doing it and not before.' Far from meaning that I was loafing or doing busy work, I in fact found myself doing the most important things I could have been doing – but without forcing myself. When I started to worry about anything, I would dismiss it by saying to myself, 'I can trust myself to know what to do and when to do it.'

The morning had taken place much as I expected, but the afternoon was different. In the hour before my client was due at 3 p.m. I did various minor tasks. These included trying to get hold of an important contact whom I needed to have a long talk with, but without success. Then at 3 p.m. my client rang to cry off. This gave me an opportunity to catch up with paperwork. And then quite unexpectedly the garage rang to tell me that my car, which had been awaiting parts for an indefinite time, was ready. So I realised that I had just time to drive the forty minutes to where the garage was situated and be back in time for my next client at six. While I was away the contact I was trying to get hold of left a message to say he would be in between 8 and 9 p.m.

Once the session with my client was finished I had supper and listened to music before ringing my contact. We had a long and useful talk and fixed up a meeting next month since he was away abroad for most of the rest of this month.

The rest of the evening I read, watched *Ab Fab* on TV, and wrote the little bit of dialogue which preceded the record of this day's events. But I did not feel like writing up the day, so didn't.

QF And you say that everything you did that day was because you felt like doing it?

A *Yes, it was all effortless in the sense of not having to push myself or overcome resistance – which doesn't mean that there was no work involved.*

QF So did your feelings lead you in ways that were expected?

A *Yes, most of the time. The morning was simply productive work. But in the afternoon I was able to react quickly to the fact that my second client cried off and that my car was ready. It's interesting that there was plenty of leisure involved. But what I didn't expect was that I* *wouldn't feel like writing the book at any time during the day. It was the first day that I haven't written a substantial amount.*

QF Did you feel resistance to it or what?

A *No, it was just the feeling that it wasn't right to do it then. It needed to be put off.*

QF So can we have a look at the following day, Saturday?

A *Yes, but the interesting thing here is that I was expecting another productive day and something wonderful to happen to finish the book off. But what I got was a day in which I basically did nothing except loaf around. In the afternoon I went and bought myself a digital camera and spent most of the rest of the day playing with it. I did no writing at all.*

QF And how did you feel about that?

A *Perfectly happy. I knew my mind was telling me that I should give things a rest for a couple of days. In the old days I would have got terribly frustrated with myself for wasting time. Now I know that I can trust my feelings.*

QF So this wasn't quite the spectacular finish that you thought your mind was preparing?

A *No.*

QF But this is a valid creation too. So what have you been creating here?

A *I have been finding out what it is to live life directly and in the moment. To be able to respond to life as I perceive it at the time, without trying to change the past or worrying about the future. This is what I think I have been aiming at all my life without being able to find it before.*

QF And how is this creation developing?

A *So many things I thought were important no longer seem to be. I now see that my true goal was to learn how to live in the present and* *appreciate what I have in the present. I see the future as an extension of the present rather than as a separate destination. The future is just a continuous series of presents, each one a development of the one before.*

QF **So since we are writing this on Sunday, let's bring our vision up-to-date.**

The vision

My vision has changed completely. Maybe I will have a castle one day, maybe I won't. But the most important thing is that I should be the person in that castle right now. That means that I am living in the moment, enjoying every minute of life, benefiting others through following my own self-interest, trusting my feelings, and knowing that above all else I am a creator. Creation flows out of me because I was created to create. And I do not create in isolation but with many others who join in the dance of creation with me. And at its widest extent that includes everyone in the entire world. I condemn no one and I am not condemned. I forgive and I am forgiven. I do not resist evil because there is no evil to resist. There is no evil or misfortune in my life because I see that everything is good.

Present Reality update

The writing of this book has been a transformative experience for me. I have passed from the desire for future wealth and fame to wanting the joy of creation for its own sake. And to knowing that I can have it now in this present time. My Present Reality *is* my Future Vision.

QF **That's wonderful. What are you going to be creating next?**

A *I don't know. I have finished the first draft of this book. I still have a lot of editing to do. Then I shall send it out into the world. Whether it will change the world I don't know. What I do know is that it has changed me.*

QF **Your aim in writing the book was to describe how to access the unconscious workings of the mind to achieve goals and life visions. What you have found is that once you have accessed the unconscious mind fully, it is its own reward and its own destination. You have found that the goals and life visions are themselves creatures of the conscious mind.**

A *I started with three methods to access the unconscious. They were the vision, the 'What's Better?' list and the dialogues. And bit by bit as I have worked through the book, I have transcended all three of them.*

QF **What is left?**

A *Simply to trust one's feelings as messengers of the unconscious mind.*

QF **To be able to do this is it necessary to go through the process you have been through?**

A *Yes, in some form. To abandon using the linear processing of the conscious mind without falling into the trap of drifting, it is necessary to find ways of integrating conscious and unconscious processing. And that is what those three methods have achieved. For most people, myself included in the past, to try to follow one's feelings without having gone through this process would be a disaster.*

QF **I think it is time for me to say goodbye.**

A *Thank you. You have served me well. And your greatest achievement is that I no longer need you.*

Monday, 1 October – Epilogue

Q It's been a long time since we last spoke. What's been better since then?

A *I've been revising the first draft of this book for publication, and that's gone well. But the interesting thing is how my mind has carried on working in the meantime.*

Q What do you mean by that?

A *I've become more aware of how some of the things in the book work and at the same time what I have written about has deepened itself in my own life.*

Q How has that worked?

A *I've found myself thinking more and more in the ways that I describe in the book. But this wasn't an instant thing, because once I'd finished the first draft it was as if I'd come out of a tunnel. Writing a book as a sort of diary is a very peculiar process because it makes you feel as if you are living your life in public. So there was a danger that when I'd finished, everything I'd kept going during that period as a sort of public performance would collapse once I was out of the public eye.*

Q And did it?

A *A little bit, yes. But what really made me stagger was that a few days after we finished the last dialogue the horrific terrorist attacks on the World Trade Center and the Pentagon took place.*

Q What effect did those terrible events have on you?

A *Like everyone else, I went through a lot of conflicting feelings. One of my earliest reactions was to query everything I'd put in this book. And I found that I had to let my feelings settle. Once I felt they had to some extent, I wrote a piece about it. It was mainly for my own benefit at the time, but I think it is important.*

---

11 September 2001

Four days after this dialogue was finished – on 11 September 2001 – the terrible terrorist attacks on the World Trade Center and Pentagon took place. These events horrified nearly the entire world and made me re-evaluate everything I had written in this book. In the end I decided to let it stand as written, but felt the need to try to put into words something of the new perspective these tragic events brought to me, as they did to so many other people around the world. My hope was that this would enable me to get deeper and deeper into the issues that this raised for me.

It is a very difficult and challenging thing to write down one's reaction to events as traumatic and horrifying as these. In the days immediately following it my mind went through an extraordinary variety of emotions. And gradually I realised that I needed to let my reactions to these events settle before making any response.

The most challenging thing to me was that I had just completed a book in which I was making statements such as that problems were opportunities for growth, that we shouldn't resist evil because we should regard nothing as evil. Faced with events so palpably evil as these how could I hold my head up and stand behind my words?

At the same time I felt it would be wrong to tear up what I had written. Accordingly I just put the draft to one side and waited for two weeks to see how my feelings would take me. And bit by bit things began to solidify out of the fog. First, I became convinced that the way to resolve these issues in my own mind was to use the methods in the book, particularly to explore the issues using the different parts of myself which feature in what has been written so far. And secondly, and more long-term, I realised that the events had thrown the really important things of life into strong silhouette. I was more determined than ever not to allow trivial things to take over. If setbacks and disasters are the times when the greatest growth is made, what were the points of growth for me?

Out of the disaster for Americans seemed to be coming a renewed sense of what it means to be American, and also a renewed sense of precisely what the value was of the freedoms and way of life that the terrorists were attacking. And the rest of the world too seemed to be coming to a similar realisation. At the end of the day, it is about a renewed sense of what one stands for, what one is all about.

I realised that this was precisely what I needed to find in these terrible events myself – a renewed sense of what I am really about and what I stand for. And I realised afresh that human beings are essentially processors of chaos, bringers of meaning to the world. We can no more expect events and circumstances to be as we want them to be than a machine for extracting gold from rocks would expect to find itself working on pure gold without the rocks. Our job is to bring meaning to reality. Without the raw material we would have nothing to do.

Another realisation I came to was that even in our normal everyday lives a degree of disorder is desirable. The perfectly ordered life is also a sterile life. In fact the perfectly ordered life resembles nothing so much as the linear conscious processing of the brain. A degree of disorder reflects far better the more holistic unconscious processing that is deeper and more powerful. And once we realise and accept that disorder is a tool to be used we are able to live with it much more powerfully than if we are continually fighting it.

All this has taken me rather far from the American tragedies. But when I ask myself whether their effect on *me* will be for good or for evil, I can see that their effect on me will be good if I allow it to be.

At this moment of writing, two weeks after the events, I feel a strong call to start again. Rather as I started again with this book, so I feel the need to start again on a wider canvas. And I feel that that will give me a renewed purpose and energy just as starting again on the book did. There was nothing wrong with my life before. And that is precisely what was wrong with it.

So the American events challenged deeply what I had written, but also, paradoxically, are becoming its validation. It is impossible not to be deeply affected and also to be apprehensive of what may still lie in the future. But it is also impossible not to be aware of the signs of growth and to sense the powerful sense of unity that these events have brought about. I would have done anything in my power to prevent these events happening. But now that they have, it behoves me to learn and apply the lessons that they have for me.

Q So you are beginning to make sense of these events, or at least make sense of them as far as they affect *you*?

A *Yes, but I think I would prefer to say that I am beginning to bring meaning to them – or perhaps again it would be better to say that I am beginning to bring meaning* out *of them for myself. Obviously the meaning that I bring out of them will be different from anyone else's meaning. I don't personally know anyone who was directly affected by these events and I can hardly imagine what it would be like for those who were.*

Q And the events too would have had an entirely different meaning for those responsible – the terrorists themselves?

A *Yes, perhaps that is an impossible thing – to attempt to understand what was in the minds of the terrorists. But one thing we can be sure of is that it made sense to them. I wrote another piece to try to understand better.*

What one can say is that this was a creation. Someone's deliberate creation. And to them it must have made sense. However much we may find it impossible to put ourselves in the place of people who would crash an aircraft full of passengers into a building full of innocent people, we have to acknowledge that it must have made sense to them. And what is more, they themselves did not see themselves as wicked but as martyrs to a noble cause. The horrific truth is that they saw themselves as good. And what is more, their motivation was love – love for God, love for their cause, love for their brothers, love for those they saw as persecuted by the forces of capitalism and godlessness. We have a desperate desire to see them as wicked men motivated by hate. But the truth is that they saw themselves as good men motivated by love. This is almost more terrifying for us to grasp because goodness and love are what we see as the defining qualities that distinguish us from them.

'Love' is dangerous medicine. I remember years ago reading somewhere: 'If you want to know what people do for love, read the murder columns in the newspapers.' I myself have heard a woman tell a man that she loved him so much that she would kill him if he left her.

'Love' too often means taking. We love someone or something not because we wish them well but because we are gaining our own self-validation from them. So love becomes a game of taking and bribing for the cause of external validation. The terrorists gave their lives not for themselves but for the sake of what they perceived as a greater cause. They were brought up to sacrifice themselves for something 'greater' than themselves. In the list of characteristics of people who act out of their own self-interest on pages 146–7, the idea of sacrificing oneself for a greater cause is conspicuously absent.

Those who are internally validated, those for whom their own being is their greatest cause, give because they wish to give and for no other reason, not for the sake of getting anything, but simply because giving is an expression of themselves. And they do not take, they receive. Giving and receiving v. bribing and taking. These are the signs of those who have truly made the connection with their own being.

Q This is the difference between loving your neighbour as yourself and loving your neighbour more than yourself?

A *Yes, these terrible perversions of love all stem from confusing the two. Whenever we are asked to sacrifice ourselves for a cause outside ourselves, we are immediately beginning to pervert what love is really about.*

Q You said earlier in the book that one of the main factors in how we relate to other people is the extent to which we share a common vision with them?

A *Yes, I did, and I think that's one of the areas in which I have learnt most. I realised that sharing a vision with other people brings them into a closer relationship, but that attempting to impose a vision on them is highly destructive. The terrorists saw Western society as imposing a vision on them that they did not want, and in return they attempted to impose their own vision by force.*

Q Too many visions have been imposed in history?

A *Yes, but what I've begun to realise is that the remedy is for each individual to be clear about their own vision for themselves. Then we can begin to build on what we share instead of destroying each other over the bits that we don't share.*

Q So you have come to see that what you are saying in this book about creating a vision for oneself is even more important than you originally thought?

A *Yes, it is essential.*

Q Why then is it so uncommon for people to have developed their own clear vision?

A *I think there are some very good reasons for it. One is that our brains construct their goals in a very efficient manner from our childhood experiences, education and later life, but left to themselves these goals tend to be* reactions *to the outside world. There has to come a time when we make the fundamental decision to take control by making our own goals.*

Q So you are saying that everyone is working under some sort of vision already, whether they know it or not?

A *Yes, but usually not one that they have deliberately constructed for themselves.*

Q Are there other reasons?

A *Yes, a second reason would be that, probably for cultural and historical reasons, our conscious logical linear processing has been given too much emphasis. We are taught almost from the cradle to think logically and* *to suppress our feelings. This has tended to mean that we are trying to run our lives using an instrument that was never designed for the job. Linear thinking is a specialist instrument designed for solving particular types of problems. It's not designed for the business of integrating and giving meaning to huge masses of raw information.*

Q That's the job of our unconscious minds?

A *Yes. I've talked a lot about 'conscious' versus 'unconscious' thinking, but the purpose of all I am saying in this book is to bring our holistic unconscious thinking more into our conscious awareness – to make us more aware of it, learn to trust it, and of course learn how to be able to target it better.*

Q One thing that interests me is that at the end of the main dialogue you had arrived at a different vision from the one you started out with. Yet I didn't get the impression that you had entirely abandoned the previous vision?

A *No, you are right. What I felt the need of was a deeper vision, one if you like that was a more or less permanent statement of what I was about. That didn't involve abandoning the three to five year vision – just putting it into a deeper context.*

Q So you are in fact working on both visions?

A *Yes. I look at them both regularly, but most of my day-to-day vision work is on short-term goals. They are always linked with the wider visions. So it's like focusing in and focusing out. I look at the whole picture, then focus in on some detail, then another, then focus out to the wider picture again. The important thing is that the more detailed goals should always be linked into the wider vision.*

Q So in that way they are always working as a unity?

A *Exactly. And as I get more and more in control of the process, so I have more and more fun just enjoying making things happen. It's like having a magic wand that actually works. That, of course, can be a bit frightening. When you know that what you ask for will happen, you have to be very careful what you ask for.*

Q I suppose you do!

A *I often used to think when I was working with churches that the only reason the congregations prayed some prayers was because they were certain they wouldn't get answered!*

Q Can you give an example?

A *Yes, there was one that was prayed every week without fail. 'Send us out in the power of your Spirit to live and work to your praise and glory.' I used to think, 'Wow! If they thought for a moment that might get answered, how many would still be praying it?'*

Q So you have to be sure to be really aware of the implications of what you are asking for?

A *Yes. Which is why it is so important to keep working on your goals and vision in the ways I have outlined in this book. You need to test them so that they are what you really want.*

Q What happens if someone tries everything in your book but still has no idea what they want out of life?

A *In that case the best thing for them to do would be to use the Goal Achievement Method on short-term goals so that they are getting more and more confident in their own power to achieve things. Then they may find that a longer-term vision develops of its own accord. Generally speaking I believe it's better to work from long-term vision down to short-term goals, but there's no law that says it has to be done that way!*

Q If you had just one thing to say to close this book, what would it be?

A *Enjoy the process. Have fun finding out what you are capable of!*

Resolve to be thyself; and know that he
Who finds himself loses his misery!
(Matthew Arnold, from 'Self Dependence')

A step-by-step course to implement the message of this book

Because this book is not structured in the conventional way, readers may find it useful to have a suggested step-by-step sequence in which they can work systematically through the methods described. I would stress that this is not the only sequence you can follow – the methods will work whatever order you take them in – but it does follow a logical progression. I would also stress that there is no laid-down or correct timescale. The dialogues given in the book only cover a period of a few weeks, but it is important to remember that I had been actively engaging with developing the methods for many months before the dialogues started. So as always it is important to go at one's own pace and not try to rush the process.

Stage One – Implementation

- Start a daily 'What's Better?' list as described in **From problem solving to growth**, page 14.
- Work through the exercises in **The Goal Achievement Method**, page 30.
- Practise the methods on a variety of very short-term goals.

- Use the **Self-coaching techniques** on pages 70–1 to start a daily self-coaching dialogue.
- Write a long-term vision (three to five years) for yourself using the exercises in **The future** on page 80. Work on it daily at first, then less often once you feel it has 'taken'.

Stage Two – Consolidation

Continue in a pattern along these lines:

Daily
- Write up your 'What's Better?' list every evening and/or keep a running list throughout the day.
- Write a self-coaching dialogue, preferably first thing.
- As required, work on short-term goals.

Weekly
- Revise your long-term (three to five year) vision and update its Present Reality.

Stage Three – Development

Be prepared to allow the self-coaching process to develop new methods that suit you better (see **Role play – Janet**, page 58). Don't worry if this never happens!

Be prepared for a deeper vision of yourself to emerge, which you can use in place of or in addition to your three to five-year vision. Don't force this – allow it to happen in its own time.

Additional

At any stage you may want to experiment with the exercises contained in **The present** (page 113) and **The past** (page 125).

How to contact the author

If you are interested in any of the following:

- becoming one of my coaching clients (limited vacancies available),
- my schedule of classes and seminars,
- subscribing to my free weekly e-mail newsletter,

then you can find up-to-date details on my website at www.markforster.net. Alternatively you can contact me direct by telephone on 01403 250016 or by e-mail at MarkForster@aol.com